"William Larkin's *Get* [...] that shows the very r[...] holiness. It is written ι∪ι ρ∪∪ρ∪ ... [...] struggling to live more harmoniously with others and with ourselves. Rather than offering pious platitudes, however, Larkin shows us how to confront our dark side and move beyond it into a realistic appreciation of ourselves and the world. His book is a 'must-read' for the wisdom it contains."

Edward Sellner
Author, *Soul-Making: The Telling of a Spiritual Journey*

"Dr. William Larkin's therapeutic intent has always been guided by the learning process of self-esteem, which he carefully delineates as the human person made to the image and likeness of God. As one reads this outstanding book, Dr. Larkin practically demonstrates that we know, love, and grow in esteem as we become more God-conscious; other-conscious, and less self-conscious. This coupling of therapy with scripture and prayer is effective when one works at it. Doctor Larkin's outstanding and effective record as a therapist proves this.

"This book presents a practical and sound psychological and theological approach to growth in self-esteem, knowing and loving the journey of being made to God's image and likeness."

Rev. Msgr. Andrew Cusack, Ph.D.
Seton Hall University

"Dr. Larkin provides a simple test by which we can quickly score our self-esteem. He then guides us through 25 chapters that move us into positive action, repetition, reflections, and prayer. His practical application and biblically rooted principles help us grow in holiness and increase our self-esteem. This book can help us improve our self-esteem and achieve our life goals. "

William J. Metzger, M.S.W.
Christian Therapist

"The author of *Get Real About Yourself* has a unique ability to blend pragmatic aspects of human development with the deeper realities of the spiritual life. The reflections on Scripture and the prayer at the end of each chapter enhance the text immensely. The book was helpful to me; I believe it will prove to be helpful to many. I highly recommend it."

Louis D. Horvath, Administrator
Villa St. John Vianney Hospital

"Dr. Larkin's practice incorporates spirituality and psychotherapy. He shows that there cannot be complete psychological healing without spiritual awareness. The spiritual side of our psychological make-up is often ignored. However, it is through this psycho-spiritual marriage that we find true peace.

"The Self-Esteem Inventory provides a sound basis from which to identify psychological conditions and addictions. Provided that this test is taken honestly and accurately, anyone can learn to deal with the negative emotions that prevent us from becoming the person that God intends us to become."

Tim Halloran
Breakthrough Producer

"Finally there is a work on self-esteem that makes sense! Dr. Larkin has managed to combine psychological understandings of the human person with concrete growth steps in the context of scripture and prayer. It is a textbook, a work manual, and a prayer book all in one. What makes this work compelling and different from many of the books on self-esteem is that Dr. Larkin has explored the fundamental issues of living always in the context of God's working in and through our human lives."

Katie Kelley, Ph.D.
Grace Institute

GET REAL
about Yourself

25 Ways to Grow Whole and Holy

WILLIAM LARKIN

TWENTY-THIRD PUBLICATIONS
Mystic, CT 06355

Twenty-Third Publications
185 Willow Street
P.O. Box 180
Mystic, CT 06355
(203) 536-2611
800-321-0411

ISBN 0-89622-606-9
Library of Congress Catalog Card Number 94-60341
Printed in the U.S.A.

To my children
whose hearts of love
have enabled my own self-esteem:

Sharon Lynn
Michele Rene
Mary Elizabeth
Christopher Michael
William Anthony

Acknowledgments

I wish, first of all, to acknowledge my patients whose lives and stories have affected the formation of not only this book, but of my life as well. This includes the many who have followed the development of this work on my radio and television programs and have taken the time to write and to express their gratitude and ideas.

Several faithful friends have provided that rare kind of moral support and confidence in me that has encouraged me, enabling me to be "believed in" when the going got rough. Special and deep thanks to Ann and Tony Massini, Mollie and Frenchy Menard, Sharon Totz and my friend on the other side of the veil of death, the late Bill Totz. They are rare people whose friendship has been a blessing to me.

The development of the original *Self-Esteem Manual*, the predecessor of this volume, was greatly aided by Rev. John Sibel. His work with the Communications Office and the Continuing Education program of the Archdiocese of Philadelphia was superior and more far-sighted than any I have seen since. I am deeply grateful to him.

Many of the ideas in this book germinated at the Archdiocese of Philadelphia and their Delaware Valley Office for Radio and Television as a part of my radio program, "Breakthrough." It has been produced with the fine help of Anne McGlone, Adrienne Daily, Joe O'Neil, and Tim Halloran. I also want to thank Marie Kelly who keeps the ship afloat.

Many of these ideas developed at the Summer Institute for Priests sponsored by Seton Hall University in South Orange, N.J. It was Msgr. Andrew Cusack's request for a measurement tool for self-esteem, and the opportunity to put these notions to the test statistically and otherwise, that led to the Inventory you'll find in these pages. A request for a follow-up program led me to develop the *Home Workshop Manual* and the Self-Esteem Seminars. Msgr. Cusack's work with self-esteem is considered a hallmark of excellence within the Catholic church, and it has been a privilege to be included in his programs.

The work on oppression and the five cycles of the "roller coaster," while quite different, were influenced by the ideas of Dr. Albert Levis. His book, *Conflict Analysis: The Formal Theory of Behavior*, while quite different theoretically from this book, is available from Normative Publications, Manchester Village, VT 05254.

David Amirault, Kimberly Boyce, and Miriam Murphy were a great help in the preparation of the orignal manuscript.

My friends Drs. Helmuth and Evelyn Gahbauer and Ann and Tony Massini often generously provided a secluded place where I could work in peace.

It would be difficult to express how much my wife Dot's love, deep belief, and support of me and this project have influenced bringing it to birth. Thank you, my dear.

Contents

Introduction

A Tool to Measure Process

Get Real About Yourself is a book about holiness and self-esteem. You can't have one without the other. Holiness is very much akin to humility, which simply means being who you are as best you can. This includes all of your "dirt," because the root word of humility is *humus*, Latin for dirt. A good deal of the time, self-esteem has more do with how you treat your "dirt," that is, the negative or shadow side of yourself, than with all the wonderful things you have accomplished or with what a good person you think you may be.

The self-esteem books that fill the shelves of bookstores today often ignore a basic reality, that it is only God who can save us from our "dirt" and resurrect us to the true self-esteem that is not built upon the sand of wonderful accomplishments or the accumulation of goods or degrees. All of these things can be taken from us. But what can never be taken from us is the love of Christ, which is the root of all true self-esteem.

Christian life is full of admonitions of self-sacrifice, but you cannot truly sacrifice a self you do not love. The result of attempting it is hostility. Many of our church leaders and members of the clergy and religious orders are full of the hostility that has resulted from sacrificing themselves out of guilt and low self-esteem. Many marriages are full of the hostility that emerges from sacrificing so much, from self-hate and self-disgust. Self-sacrifice not based on self-esteem just doesn't work, and the web that self-hate spins can trap, or at least affect, all who come close, especially those within our care and those we love the most.

This book is adapted from a much larger work called *The Self-Esteem Manual* which was written for use in teaching seminars and for counselors. This abbreviated and adapted edition is designed to be more usable and workable in an everyday sense for the everyday person.

Get Real About Yourself contains an adaptation of the Self-Esteem Inventory which you are strongly encouraged to take before you begin to work through this book. It is not an absolute measure of self-esteem, but merely an indicator of how you might tend to undermine your self-esteem during difficult times in your life.

Self-esteem is not a constant; it is also not a given, something you either have or don't have. Self-esteem, rather, is something you learn and cultivate all of your life, something you can lose track of during your journey through life. This book is designed to help you stay on track and rediscover your self-esteem.

It is important that you work through Chapters 1-5 of this book first. They introduce you to the most fundamental concepts of self-esteem and also to the "roller coaster of addiction." We are all addicted to some thing or some pattern of living when our self-esteem is either threatened or low. These first five chapters will also introduce you to the "roller coaster of healthy coasting," which can lead to a perception of self-esteem that helps ensure a healthier person. After Chapters 1-5, you can jump around as chapters seem to interest you, or you can read and work straight through the book in the given sequence.

The original 102-question Self-Esteem Inventory was tested with patients in private practice. In addition, 365 members of Alcoholics Anonymous took the test, an entire archdiocese of over 900 priests went through the Self-Esteem Seminar, and the National Institute for Priests participated in two studies. The use of the *Self-Esteem Manual* produced highly significant statistical results in self-esteem scores. This shorter version, *Get Real About Yourself*, is based upon these results and has been designed for your use.

The Self-Esteem Inventory

Take this test now. After you read each item, or statement, circle the number with each statement that best describes you right now: "1" is least true; "10" is most true. When you have completed the test, score yourself by using the guide on pages 5-6.

1. I often feel that things are getting the best of me, rather than that I am in control of them.
1 2 3 4 5 6 7 8 9 10

2. I am able to trust others.
1 2 3 4 5 6 7 8 9 10

3. I believe that people like me.
1 2 3 4 5 6 7 8 9 10

4. I know what my goals are.
1 2 3 4 5 6 7 8 9 10

5. I get the job done, but people don't usually really like me.
1 2 3 4 5 6 7 8 9 10

6. I am able to listen to criticism.
1 2 3 4 5 6 7 8 9 10

7. If people knew what I was really like, they would be disappointed.
1 2 3 4 5 6 7 8 9 10

8. Every once in a while, I have to do something to let people know that I am not so "holy."
1 2 3 4 5 6 7 8 9 10

9. When conflict occurs, I deal with it in an appropriate time frame.
1 2 3 4 5 6 7 8 9 10

10. I would describe myself as stubborn.
1 2 3 4 5 6 7 8 9 10

11. I get my way more often than I give in to others.
1 2 3 4 5 6 7 8 9 10

12. It is difficult for me to ask for help.
1 2 3 4 5 6 7 8 9 10

13. I tend to be the accommodating person.
1 2 3 4 5 6 7 8 9 10

14. I am able to be dependent upon significant others.
1 2 3 4 5 6 7 8 9 10

15. I am in touch with my real needs.
1 2 3 4 5 6 7 8 9 10

16. I like to have the last word.
1 2 3 4 5 6 7 8 9 10

17. I always respect and obey rules and regulations.
1 2 3 4 5 6 7 8 9 10

18. I keep my anger well controlled and guarded.
1 2 3 4 5 6 7 8 9 10

19. I have difficulty facing conflict; I usually run away from things.
1 2 3 4 5 6 7 8 9 10

20. As I look back over my life, things add up to a whole and make sense.
1 2 3 4 5 6 7 8 9 10

21. I tend not to let others know I have problems.
1 2 3 4 5 6 7 8 9 10

22. I've had enough of everything, I'm fed up.
1 2 3 4 5 6 7 8 9 10

23. When I am not successful, I "shake it off" and go on.
1 2 3 4 5 6 7 8 9 10

24. I believe that things will work out well.
1 2 3 4 5 6 7 8 9 10

25. I can make up my mind without too much trouble, and later not doubt my decision.
1 2 3 4 5 6 7 8 9 10

Self-Esteem Inventory Score

To obtain your score:

1. Add the scores you gave yourself for these Inventory numbers: 2,3,4,6,9,14,15,20,23,24,25. This is your A score.

2. Then add the scores you gave yourself for these Inventory numbers: 1,5,7,8,10,11,12,13,16,17,18,19,21,22. This is your B score.

3. Subtract your B score from your A score for your total score. *It is possible for your score to be in a negative, or minus, range.* If your B score is higher than your A score, you will automatically score in a negative or minus range. Note that it is very difficult to get a high score on the Inventory, because it seeks to measure the pull of negative influences on positive realities and to repeat the dynamics of oppression. The following is a guide for your total score.

4. Interpret your score as follows:

10 or below—You have a very strong tendency to undermine your self-esteem and to sabotage success in your life when you are oppressed.

11-30—You have a strong tendency to undermine self-esteem and sabotage your success when you are oppressed.

31-40—You are susceptible to negative influences that undermine both your self-esteem and your capacity to expect positive things in your life when you are oppressed.

41-50—While you are less susceptible to negative influences and to oppression, your self-esteem is not stable
enough that it may not waver and cause a sense of a loss of direction when you are oppressed.

51-70—While you are less susceptible to negative influences, your self-esteem is stable enough that you have a
fair amount of skill in maintaining a good self-image.

71-85—You are good at maintaining your self-esteem in the
face of negative and adverse circumstances. You do not undermine your own success; you allow yourself to experience a
certain amount of joy in your life.

86-96—You make it a point to program your life in such a
way that you maintain your high self-esteem. Whether you
identify it as such or not, you are often in a "flow" of life.
Very little gets you down, and you have learned to handle
negative influences in your life in such a way that they cannot
undermine your stable self-esteem.

Chapter Features

Each of the 25 chapters in *Get Real About Yourself* directly cor-
responds to one of the 25 items, or statements, about yourself,
in the Self-Esteem Inventory. The chapter "title" in each case
is the same as the Inventory item, and the chapter itself ex-
amines in detail what the Inventory item means.

For each item in the Inventory there is a place at the beginning of its corresponding chapter marked 1 2 3 4 5 6 7 8 9
10. Consult the Inventory to find out where you scored yourself on the "1-10 continuum"; circle that same number of the
corresponding chapter.

Each chapter is divided into five sections: Insight, Moving
Into Action, Repeating It 20 Times, Reflecting on Scripture,
and Praying.

Insight

The Insight section in each chapter will explain the rationale
behind each item, or statement about yourself. You will begin
to understand more fully the purpose of the chapter title. You

may find, in simply reading the rationale for the item, that you see the item in a different way. You may find that you differently perceive what is being asked once you have gained more insight into the item. Some of the insights will be surprising and not at all what you expected. This is important because it will make you think about yourself. You may even find that you disagree with a particular item in the Inventory and want to define self-esteem for yourself in a different way. That's all right. But see what happens to your thinking as you work through several items. Remember, this is a process measurement tool and you are engaged in a process of insight and growth.

Moving Into Action

These are exercises that can help you grow in their particular areas. One of the most often asked questions in seminars and after reading theoretical work is, "All right, now that I understand that I have low self-esteem, what do I do about it?" The problem will not be in not knowing what to do; it will be in deciding what to do first. There are hundreds of suggested ideas for growth in these pages. You may want to use some and not bother with others. Some ideas may elicit others in your own mind. If that is the case, *Get Real About Yourself* is working. Try out your own ideas for growing when they occur to you.

Repeating It 20 Times

These short statements are positive messages that you can repeat to yourself over and over again as you work through particular items during the day.

Reflecting on Scripture

For many religious people, self-esteem is anathema. It seems that their religion has taught them that it inhibits growth in spirituality. To believe that self-deprecation is actually part of spirituality is heresy. By reflecting on the selected Scripture verses, you deepen the insights you are gaining.

Praying

Part of the way to overcome low self-esteem is through prayer, encountering, in some form or other, a "higher power." Use the Scripture meditations and the prayer sections as they seem important and pertinent to you. But don't ignore them simply because you believe you are not a "religious" person. Give them a try. Christians believe that God can heal, that God answers our cries for help, especially when we determine to grow toward God and others in healthy self-esteem.

The Inventory items and corresponding chapters will make you think. They will demand self-scrutiny. They will not demand an absolutely prescribed "way" to self-esteem, but they will help you move in that direction. And if you follow the directions, you will very likely grow in self-esteem in surprising ways.

Make the Self-Esteem Inventory and *Get Real About Yourself* work for you; you are not to work for "them." Use what helps and discard what does not. What you discard at first, you may want to return to after some months. As you grow, what seemed so important in the beginning may seem insignificant months later.

This is not a test designed to tell you absolutely where you are; it is a process measurement tool to help you go where you would like to go in relation to your own self-image.

Not an Absolute Test

A word of caution: Please do not make the damaging error that we have made with intelligence testing. Once we found out what our I.Q. was, or at least what a very limited measure told us it was supposed to be, we followed it ever since and believed it to be true in an absolute sense. Traditional I.Q. tests are under great fire today and should be. Don't make this another one-time test in which the results become forever fixed in your own mind. To the absolute contrary, this Inventory is designed for the score to change and to show you how to change your score.

1

I often feel things are getting the best of me rather than that I am in control of them.

1 2 3 4 5 6 7 8 9 10

Insight

The key word in a major subset of items in this inventory is the word "oppression." Usually we think of oppression in terms of situations involving social justice. We speak of people who are oppressed. What is also true is that an individual person can be oppressed and it is a situation many of us allow.

When we say to ourselves, "I'm on top of it," we mean that in one way or another we feel that we are more or less in control of our lives and the situations that make up our lives. This sense of control and competence is essential to our sense of self-esteem. It is almost impossible to feel a sense of self-esteem if you feel overwhelmed by the events of life. How often do you feel overwhelmed? How often do you say to yourself, "I'm losing it; it's all getting the best of me"?

This is the life circumstance we will refer to as "oppression." It is a universal trait, a part of human nature, that we are designed to escape from oppression. Most of the time we see this escape as relating to larger social structures of injustice. But it is also true that no matter how much we change the social system or the environment, we can still end up feeling "oppressed."

The "Click"

Oppression is not so much something that is done to us as it is something that we do to ourselves. One of the greatest wonders of the human spirit is our capacity to endure oppression and not be overcome by it. God has not created us to be oppressed. To the contrary, the Spirit of God moves in the world and calls on us to overturn social and personal oppression. Being oppressed (or oppressing others) is quite simply not God's will for our lives. There are few, if any, structures or social systems that are free of all kinds of oppressiveness. There is a curious "click" that occurs in the human mind and in the human spirit when we say to ourselves, "I'm not on top of things; they're controlling me." At that moment we have set ourselves up to experience oppression and the necessity of finding an escape from it. This is a fundamental factor in understanding the dynamics of addictive behavior.

The Escape

We have to escape oppression, but if the escape itself is pleasurable, even if it has severe consequences, we can re-create the experience of oppression in order to experience the pleasure of escaping. Our lives are filled with addictions, from drugs to television and sex; even religion can be an addiction. Just because something looks good doesn't mean that our response to it is a sign of a healthy mind and spirit. The real force of evil works to undermine our fight against oppression because we are susceptible to sin; without the grace of God we are powerless to resist its influence.

Too often, having the experience of "it's getting the best of me" is not healthy. Most of us can handle two or three stressors in our lives. But beyond that, we probably cannot handle many more stressors at one time without feeling oppressed. We have to go away or get out from under the burden. Sometimes a single, large stressor is enough to make us feel oppressed.

We will always escape from oppression; we will always find a way to get out.

Sometimes, we can walk around for months feeling helpless and as though we have little or no control over the events of our lives—that life simply controls us. We have come to an inner realization that "it's getting the best of me."

Moving Into Action

Refer to Charts 1 and 2, My Roller Coaster of Addiction and My Roller Coaster of Healthy Coasting, on page 12-13. You will use these charts as you work through the first five items on the Inventory list. The first roller coaster begins with Oppression and moves to the left. The second begins with Challenges and moves to the right. If there is not enough room in the boxes for writing, and there will likely not be, use a separate piece of paper.

These charts are put in the suggestive form of a roller coaster for several reasons. First, the roller coaster represents the ups and downs of life. Second, these roller coasters, like real roller coasters, contain energy that is largely set in motion by the first loop. Up, up, up you go to the top of the first loop, which provides the energy to send you on your way. So it is with oppression. Oppression is the energy loop that sends us on our way through our own individual addictive cycles. This is the negative coaster of addictive cycles that undermines self-esteem. The same is true for the healthy roller coaster. A life full of challenges to be met gives us the energy to develop healthy cycles of coasting with high self-esteem through life.

Recognizing the Inner Click
In the loop that is marked #1 on Chart 1, you will see a box (Oppression) with a list marked Stress 1, Stress 2, etc. On these lines, write down the major stressors in your life, the things that you feel are on top of you, the things that get you down. Put the most important and most frequently occurring stress first. See if you can list at least eight major stressors in your life. You may need another piece of paper for this. These major issues and major involvements may not all actually be causing stress at any one time, but they are capable of doing so.

Most of us can handle one or two or three stressors at a giv-

chart 1

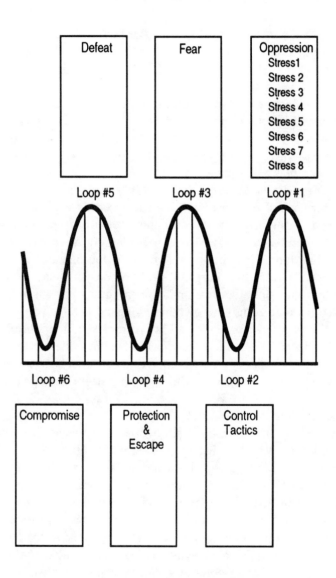

My Roller Coaster of Addiction

chart 2

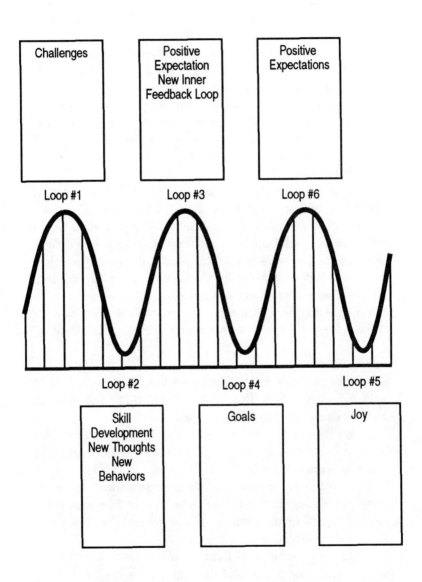

Challenges

Positive Expectation New Inner Feedback Loop

Positive Expectations

Loop #1   Loop #3   Loop #6

Loop #2   Loop #4   Loop #5

Skill Development New Thoughts New Behaviors

Goals

Joy

My Roller Coaster of Healthy Coasting

en time and still feel that we are in control. But when you cross the line, say, to stress four, or if all of these items are presently causing stress, you very well may feel oppressed and are on the first loop or box of My Roller Coaster of Addiction.

Beside each stressor that you have written, write a plus sign if the stressor is active and actually causing stress at this moment. If the stressor is present, but not an issue at this time, write a question mark; this represents the potential for the appearance or activation of this stressor in your life. For example, your job may not be a stressor at this moment, but it may be a potential stressor if the boss has a bad day or a bad week or if business is off.

You will notice that in Chart 2, My Roller Coaster of Healthy Coasting, Loop #1 is labeled Challenges. These are ways of dealing with your stressors. As you proceed through this book, you will learn multiple ways of dealing with each of the stressors you have listed. These are built into the exercises you are asked to complete in the section called Moving Into Action. There are also many resources for dealing with stress listed in Additional Resources, pages 143-144. You can list these in Loop #1 on My Roller Coaster of Healthy Coasting.

Ask Yourself

1. At what point are things getting the best of me?

2. How and when do I let the "inner click" happen that ends up causing me to feel oppressed?

3. Are there any stressors that I need to get out of my life? Are there unnecessary stressors I have allowed to remain that I need to work on to remove?

4. Have I taken upon myself so many stressors that I need to get rid of some of them? If so, which ones? Rate each stressor in terms of its importance in your life and then ask yourself if it is necessary to have it.

5. How do you respond to situations in life that may make your stressors more stressful than they really need to be? Do you allow yourself to be oppressed because you are too "controlling" or because you worry too much?

6. Do you oppress yourself to get attention?

7. Do you oppress yourself to get the pleasurable experience of escaping from it?

These are all difficult questions and you may want to discuss them with someone you trust or with a counselor, if this is a particularly problematic area of your life.

One of the most important things you can do in this area is to begin to recognize the inner click in your everyday life. Start to look for those times when you have to tell yourself "This is really getting the best of me," or when you are beginning to feel overwhelmed. You may need to learn to take things more slowly and to respond differently to stress. In what areas are you discovering that you are overwhelmed? Do you want to be controlled by this inner response, or do you want to be more in control of your life?

Whenever you feel that events are getting the best of you, jot down in a notebook where and when you are having this experience. Then at that point, or at a later time if it is not convenient when the experience happens, list all of the stressors that are going on. Rather than letting them swirl around in your head, list each stressor and grab "visual control" of them on paper. List five things you can do about each of these stressors. And if you cannot list anything to do about some of them, talk with someone, pray, and write down in that blank space, "I refuse to worry."

Practice presenting the stressors before God. So often we play god by worrying and stressing ourselves about things down the road. Eighty-five percent of what we worry about never happens. As the Lord's Prayer says, "Give us this day our daily bread," that is, the strength to deal with what we have to deal with. God gives us that strength only in 24-hour packages.

Most of the time we let ourselves be too easily controlled by stressors without even realizing what is happening to us. Most of us can have more control over our lives than we believe.

Repeating It 20 Times

I can recognize when things seem to be "getting the best of me." I can take greater control of my life.

Reflecting on Scripture

Psalm 37:1–11

These words are an almost perfect formula for not ever getting oppressed. Follow this scripture and the dynamic that most lowers self-esteem, oppression, will be conquered in your life. This may be a portion of scripture that you may want to read every day; it's a great way to start the day.

Praying

Lord, my life is not nearly so out of control as I sometimes think it is. The truth is that I sometimes worry because I don't know what else to do. And perhaps I react too quickly and too strongly to things that really don't matter all that much. Sometimes I think I enjoy making myself miserable. Most of the time, the things I dread never come to be anyway. Forgive me, Lord, for being my own worst enemy at times. Comfort me with your gift of hope. Amen.

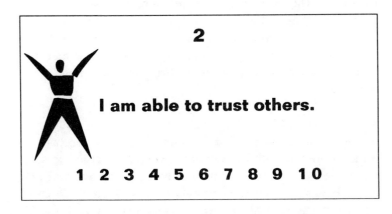

2

I am able to trust others.

1 2 3 4 5 6 7 8 9 10

Insight

There is a story of a hospital in Germany following World War II where they cared for infants who had lost parents in the war. The infant mortality rate was extremely low there and researchers wanted to find out why the infants were faring so well. After an exhaustive inquiry, the research team of doctors found no explanation for the low mortality rate, and they began to suspect that that the doctor in charge had "fudged" the statistics. As the doctors were leaving the hospital, they looked back over the ward and noticed a slightly retarded woman rocking one of the infants in the corner. One of the doctors inquired who she was. The doctor in charge responded, "Oh, that's Crazy Anna. She comes in every day and rocks the babies."

Through human touch, Anna was communicating to infants who were not otherwise touched, fondled, or rocked that the world was all right and that the infant could say yes to life. In effect, the infants were making, on a very fundamental level, a decision to surrender to life and its care-taking systems. This is the root of trust. Through the love of human hands, the love of God is communicated.

We have become aware that an infant can somehow "decide" that the world is a safe or unsafe place, and can accept

or refuse nurturance. It is the mother or the mother sur-
rogate—in this case, Anna—that is the infant's first experience
with trust. The mother and the community surrounding and
supporting that mother in her role communicate to the child
the basic trustworthiness of the nurturance of the world. On
the basis of that, the infant "decides" to take other matura-
tional steps that lead to quantum leaps in growth and perception.

The Trust to Say Yes

It is interesting that the first decision for trust is one that we
continue to make all through our lives. The decision to surrender to life and to say yes and to trust that we will get
through it all is called forth from us again and again. We learn
again and again that the trust to surrender is met by the hand
of God's love.

One of the most difficult objects of trust is people. It is people that most often let us down and do not come through for
us, who hurt us and do not nurture and take care of us in the
ways we deserve or would have liked.

Along the way, we also learn whether people can trust us,
whether we can be trusted to come through for others. We
learn, as well, whether we can trust ourselves with our
"selves."

The basic question here is not whether you can or can't
trust other people and ultimately God. The basic question is
whether you can trust yourself. Because if you can trust yourself, you can trust other people. It's as simple as that—and as
complex as that.

All of us were nurtured in ways that told us that others in
some way did not come through for us. Just as there are no
perfect children, there are no perfect parents. When this happens, there are always the "Crazy Annas" who come through
for us as though they were mysteriously sent to take care of us
just at the right time. Eventually, though, there is a line we
cross. While it is true that we must always allow others to nurture us and that we must always be dependent upon others in
healthy ways, there is a line we cross where we must become

for ourselves what "Crazy Anna" was for those infants.
It is widely known that parents who abuse their children were themselves abused as children. And so it goes with many perpetuating, generational problems. What we have yet to grasp is that the intervening factor that changes the abused into the abuser is the point at which the person begins to be a self-abuser. There is a line we cross when we take unto ourselves our own parenting; we become our own parent. Most people are harder on themselves than their parents ever were. We are oftentimes our own abusers. We can become addicted to abusing ourselves in a multitude of ways; each is typical of the person.

Trusting Ourselves
When we cross over the line and become our internal parent, we begin to take the decisive journey that will allow us to trust or not trust ourselves; to trust or not trust others. Again, if we do not trust ourselves, we will not trust others or God.

Most people take the combination of how their parents or parent surrogates treated them and apply it to themselves, especially when they feel overburdened and overwhelmed. If the rearing was positive, we see a person who is able to cope with the world in healthy and trusting ways. If it was negative and abusive, then the person will inevitably move in patterns of self-abuse and mistrust.

A key insight into the issue of self-trust is to consider how your parents controlled you or punished you when you misbehaved. Combine both of their approaches and see how you use that combination on yourself.

Moving Into Action
Write down how your parents controlled and/or punished you when you stepped out of their standard of behavior.

Can you recall times when you do to yourself what your parents did to you?

Do these times occur when you are stressed, overburdened, or when you have failed others or yourself?

Are you being fair to yourself?

Are you treating yourself in a way that enables you to trust yourself *with you*?

Write down how you would have liked your parents to treat you when you did something wrong.

Write down how you would like to treat yourself when you are stressed, overburdened, or when you make a mistake or fail.

My Roller Coaster

Turn to My Roller Coaster of Addiction, Chart 1 on page 12, and in the space marked Loop #2, write down how your parents controlled and punished you. You may need a separate piece of paper for this. In the same loop write down how you do the same thing to yourself now. Also write how you do the same thing to others. Identify how you control yourself and others in the same ways that you were controlled and punished by your parents or by those responsible for you.

Turn now to Chart 2, My Roller Coaster of Healthy Coasting, page 13. In Loop #2, write down how you would like to treat yourself when you are stressed, overburdened, and when you make a mistake or fail.

Also write down how you would like to treat others when you feel a great deal of stress. How would you like to behave more effectively toward yourself and toward others? A part of what you write here may be the positive use of the ways in which your parents controlled you. Are there ways that you can learn from them and take the best of it into your life?

Write down the last time you felt oppressed or a failure, and then write down how you treated yourself.

How did you do?

How do you believe a God of infinite love wants you to be treated and wants you to treat yourself?

What changes are you going to make? Write them down so that you can see them right in front of you.

Repeating It 20 Times

I can learn to treat myself better and to trust myself. I can trust others wisely when I am wise in trusting myself.

Reflecting on Scripture

2 Corinthians 2:5–11

In this letter to the Corinthians, St. Paul makes a profound statement of trust. He is so vitally sure that the sufferings they are all experiencing will draw them closer in community through the consolations that Christ will give. Paul knows that the Corinthians who share in Christ's sufferings will also share in his consolations and he is calling them to trust, as he trusts, in the absolute faithfulness of God. He reminds them that a death warrant is out for him and still he trusts in the God he knows will come through for him and for them. St. Paul also knows that trust is essential for faith and essential for the young Christian community that is shaky in its growth and stability.

Praying

Lord, the person I most often have to forgive is myself. The person I have to trust is myself. I am often not good to myself and blame my harshness on you and complain that you are distant. Sometimes I wonder if you even exist. At such times, I especially wonder if you exist for me. Lord, I often do to myself what I blame you for. Help me to forgive myself and love myself.

I sometimes berate myself and think that I am going to hate myself into being good. How futile and foolish. You sent your Son to live and die for me that I might be able to love myself, trust myself, and share myself with others, and I have often thwarted your most precious design by being harsh to myself.

Where I have done this in the name of religion, forgive me, Lord. Where I have done this to escape really growing up into the person you have created me to be, forgive me, Lord. Where I have bound myself up and am not free to love you, forgive me, Lord, and heal me. May I continue to grow, by your grace. Amen.

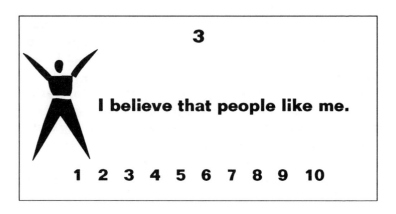

3

I believe that people like me.

1 2 3 4 5 6 7 8 9 10

Insight

If you believe that people like you, they will. If you believe that people like you, you like yourself. If you believe that God loves you, you will have a positive faith-life. What we expect, we create.

If this is something you have difficulty with, ask yourself what you do when you expect that someone won't like you. There are generally two responses at either end of a continuum: overcompensating or withdrawal.

Overcompensating
One kind of overcompensating is revealed in the form of being too ingratiating, trying too hard to please the other person. Perhaps this is done by giving gifts or by being particularly helpful, or by trying to say all the right things and in being lavish with praise and compliments, or by being too understanding, using a kind of denial that refuses to see the other person for who or what he or she really is.

Overcompensating can take another extreme. Instead of being ingratiating, you may be critical, harsh, or even mean. You may go to great lengths to keep the person you believe does not like you "in her place." You may refuse to give her any satisfaction. You may work on always having the right things to say and in always being able to "come back" at her in a split second. At least you wish you could. You may even rehearse over and over in your mind just how you would like to lash out at the person who, you believe, doesn't like you. You would really "put her in her place."

Withdrawing
At the opposite end of overcompensating is withdrawal and internalizing. You feel uncomfortable in the presence of the other person. You can't seem to open your mouth and say what you want to say. You can't stop being nervous, so you can't think of something pertinent or "bright" to add to the conversation. You may smile, nod, and speak when spoken to, but really add nothing to the conversation.

When you finally say something and contribute to the conversation, you immediately wonder if you said the right thing. You may immediately feel that you have just made a fool of yourself. You may imagine that no one heard you, or that they ignored you and went on, leaving you out of the conversation.

If you believe that other people will not like you and you handle your belief by withdrawing, basically you keep yourself locked up inside, and you fill your head with negative thoughts about how others perceive you.

Most of the time you are wrong. When you believe that other people will not like you, you have created an internal filter that will automatically interpret what other people do as *precisely not liking you.* By nature, you have to make what happens outside you agree with how you see reality on the inside. This also extends to your core beliefs about God. Otherwise, you feel as though you might be going crazy.

The truth of the matter is that not everyone is going to like you. *Not everyone is going to like you! There, it's out!* Now you can go on and be concerned about most of the people out there who *will* like you—especially if you decide to like yourself. The only one who will love you unconditionally, no matter what you are like, is God.

Moving Into Action

Decide that you will believe that people like you until such time as you have absolute hard facts that they do not. Decide that you will stop interpreting, reading into, and surmising from a "remark" that you are not liked. Let it be the other person's problem, unless the person who doesn't like you gives you hard evidence that such is the case. You are probably not as intuitive as you think you are.

If that happens, decide if you want to do something about the situation, or go on to other people who will like you. At this juncture of journeying into self-esteem, you are going to simply go on and not worry about the people who don't like you. That can be their problem, not yours. There are too many fish in the sea to allow a few people who may or may not like you—for reasons that are probably far more likely their own than yours—to get in your way and bog you down. So decide to go on with life, your life and your life with God.

After you decide that you will believe that people will like you, you have to make another important decision. You will also have to decide to like more people and to be more tolerant. You will stop scratching people off your list because of this or that. This is most important. Not only will you decide to like other people, you are also going to decide to overlook most of their faults and to let their faults be their business, not yours. You may need to take this kind of letting go to prayer and let God aid you in this step.

Reshaping Your Thinking

Begin to reshape the way you think about yourself. To do so, recognize seven ways of thinking that get you in trouble:

- Dumping
- Mirror "Yuk"
- Fat Freckle
- Aged
- Dumb and Boring
- Too Muching
- Loner

These are labels for ways of thinking that lead you ultimately to decide that other people won't like you. The tendency in dealing with a problem of believing that people don't like you is to look for the underlying cause. Forget the underlying cause. If there is one, let's just pretend for the next year that there isn't one. What *is* the problem is the way you think negatively about yourself and the habit you have gotten yourself into. That's what's wrong: your thinking about yourself!

Dumping
Dumping is defined here as taking all the blame for everything on yourself. If you hadn't done this, then that wouldn't have happened. If you had only done this or that, then this or that would have happened and everything and everyone would be wonderful. Dumping is the quickest way of resolving a conflict because you take all the blame. Actually, dumping everything on yourself doesn't resolve a thing.

Dumping is the kind of thinking that tells you, for example, that you ruined everything on your last date, that when the conversation got boring or slow, you should have jumped in with something bright and witty. It doesn't occur to you that you shouldn't have to be "on" all the time during a date or a meeting. Be quiet and let other people squirm a little. Let other people share the responsibility of keeping things "going" and interesting. But don't you take all the blame.

Another example. He asked you where you wanted to go. You asked him where he wanted to go and he said, "No, let's go where you want to go." So you went and it was terrible. The food was insipid, the atmosphere was brash, and the check was too high. Of course, you offered to pay, but you weren't allowed. And so you dump the whole thing on yourself rather than thinking that if the other person asked you where you wanted to go, the other person also had the responsibility of taking the consequences or of being more thoughtful and coming up with a good suggestion himself.

But no, you are the world's dumping ground. If anyone has any garbage, your psyche has become the town emotional dump. When you can't fix everyone's problem or can't make everyone feel better, it's your fault. When they won't let you place blame on them, or don't want to listen to your problems, you end up telling yourself that you're selfish and inconsiderate and expect too much of other people.

There is a reverse side to taking all the blame: denying that you are responsible. If something doesn't work, you assure everyone that it is not your responsibility, but inside you secretly place all the blame on yourself.

Recognize those instances when you are taking all the blame. Also recognize when you are failing to take responsibility because you are actually afraid the whole thing really is your fault. Don't place the blame all on yourself—share it.

Mirror "Yuk"

This is what happens when you look in the mirror at a time when you know you shouldn't, when you are at your worst and saying to yourself that deep inner "Yuk." Many people who believe that people don't like them will actually look at themselves in the mirror and convince themselves that there is reason for that kind of thinking. "Yuk," they say about themselves. At one time or another, all of us can do that. However, you can make such a habit out of it that even when you look good, you think you look bad.

First of all, people don't look at you nearly as closely or as critically as you look at yourself. From now on, when you look in the mirror you must say, "I love you and I like you, and so does God." Then smile at yourself five times and say your friendliest hello. This sounds corny, but just do it. You have to practice. You have to tell your feelings and your negative thoughts that they are not the boss. You are, and you have decided that you are likeable and that other people are likeable too. Remember, every time you forget and look in the mirror and say anything like "yuk," apologize and smile not five, but ten times, saying, "I like you."

So, no more of this negative attitude. Give this approach a try—for yourself and for those around you whom you've been given to appreciate. Putting yourself down is an insult to God's creation.

Fat Freckle

Everyone has a fat freckle of one kind or another. Some time ago, I was watching a talk show about cosmetic facial surgery. The man on the program had gotten his nose shortened. I thought it was a shame, because in my eyes he looked better with his nose the way it was.

I know that there are cases where changes by facial surgery have made a great difference in the lives of people. However, much of the time, this is an expensive way of dealing with a problem I call "fat freckle." The problem is not the "fat freckle" or the "flab" or the balding or the mole on your cheek. The problem is how you make this physical defect all of you. It becomes the only thing you can see, the only thing you can concentrate on. You blow it out of proportion and use it as a reason not to like yourself. "Fat freckle" thinking does not take the whole you into consideration. You are much more than this physical defect.

Aged

This is the kind of thinking that believes that because you are "aging," you are less desirable. You may be less desirable to an 18 year old, but then again, you may not be. When you begin to think that people either younger or older will not like you because of age, recognize that negative kind of thinking for what it is: aged thinking. Very often the exact opposite is true. When you think "aged" thoughts, stop them and change them. I'll explain how after we have described the seven thoughts. We are about to witness a revolution in our attitude toward aging in this country. As our lifespan increases, our view of it will be radically changed as we adapt to a new one-third or even a new one-half of life. This may be God's greatest gift to the twentieth century: more time to enjoy creation.

Dumb and Boring

Learn to recognize any thought in which you are telling yourself that you lack intelligence or that you are boring. Whenever you tell yourself anything like that, "catch the thought." Recognize that you are thinking this way. This is half the battle:

knowing that it is going on and that you are doing something to counteract it. Are you cooperating with this thought by believing it is true? Just because you think it doesn't make it true.

Too Muching

This is like "fat freckle." It's the kind of thinking that tells you that you are not liked because you are always too much of this and not enough of that. It comes from making a comparison with a standard that you haven't identified. Just what is the standard against which you are measuring yourself? There is a problem in causality here. It does not follow that even if you are too much this or that, that people won't like you. Remember, you can't judge whether or not you are liked until you have the absolute facts.

"Too muchers" are also usually "whiners," and you may be using this kind of thinking as an excuse to avoid people because you believe you will be rejected. Everyone who takes the risk of entering a relationship and of liking and being liked is going to be rejected one way or another many times. Join the human race and stop escaping by "too muching" yourself into isolation.

Loner

Many people who need friends but believe that they will not be liked give themselves the insurance policy of calling themselves "a loner." There is a part in all of us that needs to be a loner; we need time by ourselves. However, to tell yourself that you are a loner when you actually need people and need to be close to people, at least a few, can lead to great self-deception. "Loner" thinking is not so much being alone as it is avoiding social interaction because you are not sure how to behave and what to say. You are not alone in that respect; everyone has to learn how to be social. It doesn't come naturally; it is a skill that is easier for some people to develop. You are responsible for learning to be social even when you would rather hide and avoid social contact. Don't fool yourself into thinking that you are a loner when the reality is that you are simply afraid.

If you scored low on this Inventory item, memorize these seven kinds of thinking that can isolate you from people who would like to be your friends or grow closer to you. Once you have memorized them, make a mark on a sheet of paper when you catch yourself thinking in these ways. Write down the one or two kinds of thinking that you most often do. Ask yourself if this makes sense. Change your negative thoughts to positive ones.

For example, if you notice that all you can see on a particular day is your "fat freckle," tell yourself that this is only one small part of who you are, that no one is as interested in it as you are.

Thought Stopping

When you find yourself thinking in any one of these seven ways, recognize the thought by getting hold of it. You will already have deflated some of its power by taking increased control of the way you think. Then tell yourself what you have decided: "I have decided to believe that people like me. I have decided to like myself. I have decided to like more people. And I will."

My Roller Coaster

On Chart 1, My Roller Coaster of Addiction (page 12), read again what you put in Loop #2, Control Tactics. These were the ways that you were controlled and punished and the ways in which you exercise control in order to escape feeling "oppressed." What you put in Loop #2 you learned from parents and from those who were responsible for you. It comprises the first earliest ways in which you learned to be in control and the ways in which you combined how your parents did it.

In Loop #3, Fear, based upon what you wrote in Loop #2, write down your fears of how others will control or punish you. Based upon the way you behave, what do you fear will eventually happen to you? Who will do to you what you do to others and how will they do it? *This may be difficult because this is usually subconscious material and you may need to give your response to the question some time to emerge. It also contains some* of our deepest beliefs about how God really regards us and what God will ultimately do to us.

How does what you have written in Loop #3 relate to your belief about whether people will like you? Usually Loop #3 is the subconscious beliefs, based upon the behavior described in Loop #2, about what will eventually happen to you. These beliefs and projections, based on your own behavior, set you up to believe that people will not or do not like you.

Now turn to Chart 2, My Roller Coaster of Healthy Coasting (page 13). In Loop #2, you wrote how you would like to behave when you are stressed and oppressed. You described how you would like to be in control in healthy ways that are an authentic expression of you as you really are.

Building upon what you wrote in Loop #2, write in Loop #3 how you expect people to respond to you. Based upon your positive behavior listed in Loop #2, write in Loop #3 how you expect the same results for yourself from others. You are beginning to predict what you will believe about others and about yourself.

Repeating It 20 Times
I have decided to believe that people like me. I have decided to like myself. I have decided to like more people. And I will.

Reflecting on Scripture
Psalm 12
The psalmist here sounds like many of my patients. "There is no one I can trust," or "No one likes me." This is usually no more true for my patients than it is for the psalmist who is obviously feeling very sorry for himself. Actually the psalm is meant to say more about how much we can trust Yahweh than that there are no trustworthy people left. The secret of the psalm is a precious one, though, because whenever we begin to trust that people like us, that trust grows. Trust is essential to life and to every human relationship. We may feel that there are times when God is the only one we can trust. However, God will lead us to see that we can trust people and that we are likeable for who and what we are.

Praying

Lord, sometimes my thinking is as bleak as that of the psalmist. I look around and can see only people I cannot or do not want to trust or believe in. But I can trust you, and in trusting you, I can come to believe that you will send me people I can trust and who will like me. Very often the person that you really want to send to me is my real self, as you have made me. If I trusted and believed in myself more, I would be more aware of others.

Lord, I am often worse to myself than others begin to be. Too often I have believed that I will not be liked because I have spent too much time not liking others and I have used this as an excuse for not giving myself to your world and to your creation. Lord, give me the grace to see what is likeable in myself and with this self-esteem like others more. Amen.

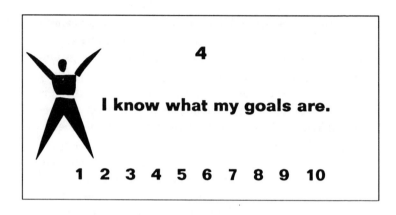

4

I know what my goals are.

1 2 3 4 5 6 7 8 9 10

Insight

Goals are plans, the outcome of positive thinking. The only people who set goals are people who absolutely believe they will meet them. To be more accurate, there are goal-setters who deceive themselves into believing that they will be able to reach unrealistic goals. This Inventory item deals with setting genuine, realistic goals that we expect to meet. People who think and believe positively set goals and work to reach them. They are also goals that we believe are congruent with God's plan for our lives.

The most important step in reaching goals is clearly and concretely setting them in the first place. If you know with some precision what your goals are in life, you have won more than half the battle of achieving them.

One of the reasons people don't set goals is because goal-setting can be limiting, that is, we will have to reject some possibilities in order to obtain others. Goals act as reins that limit us in our decisions, telling us what we may and may not do. Although goals give us directions important for security, they also remove a certain amount of freedom because, as we set realistic goals, we will have to be disciplined enough to say no to whatever doesn't bring us closer to attaining them.

Sabotaging Success

Achieving our goals will take work, discipline, consistency, perseverance, and the positive expectation that we will obtain them. Setting goals also means believing that we deserve to achieve them. Often, the closer people come to attaining their goals, the more they will sabotage their success, because they believe subconsciously that they don't deserve the attainment of the goals they have set. We may think we don't deserve and should not have the good things God wants to give us. God wants to share creation and wants us to enjoy it.

Goal-setting is an important indication of high self-image and high self-esteem. People with high self-esteem have invariably set goals and persevered in reaching them; they have claimed and made their accomplishments their own. Goal achievement and high self-esteem—each feeds upon the other.

It should be noted that accomplishments in and of themselves do not give us a sense of self-esteem and self-confidence because many of these successes can be taken from us.

While goals must always remain flexible and changeable, it is important that they be set in realistic increments. That is to say, achieving goals is a process of setting three-month, six-month, one-year, two-year, and five-year goals. These goals always have to be reevaluated, particularly the two- and five-year goals, in the light of our success with the shorter-term goals. Having achieved these intermediate goals may tell us more about ourselves and will very likely point new directions, or adjustments, for achievement and satisfaction.

One of the most common complaints I hear from people I ask to set goals is that they don't have the time to do it, or that even when they do, events work in such a way that they can never achieve their goals. It seems that something is always interrupting their pursuit, or something is always changing the goals they've set, and they have come to believe that whether or not they set goals, they will not be able to achieve them. In effect, what these people are doing is oppressing themselves by their own thinking. Goal-setting also means altering the nature of circumstances around us so that we can accomplish our goals.

It is important to realize that some goals may not be attained right away and that we may have to learn to wait. It may be realistic that some goals may not be achieved in five or ten years, or that we might not even be able to begin striving for some goals until fifteen or eighteen years down the road. This does not mean, however, that it's unimportant to set long-range goals and keep an eye on them.

Also, setting and achieving goals is never truly an isolated affair, but rather a team effort. Goals are not entirely isolated events in our lives. They are influenced by and are the products of our relationships with others; they are always shared realities. While we talk a great deal these days about "doing things for myself" and "being good to myself," the capacity to do so depends upon a healthy interaction with one's community.

If the team around you constantly thwarts you from reaching your goals, it may be important to seek outside help in order to bring about changes in yourself and your environment that will allow you to move forward in the pursuit of your goals. Along the way there may have to be many adjustments, compromises, and changes, and there will be many expectations and lost expectations. The important point is to set the goals, and if they prove to be unrealistic or unobtainable, to set more obtainable and realistic ones. Not to set goals because others seem to be getting in the way—there's a poor excuse for dealing with life.

Moving Into Action

The first part of this behavioral assignment is to go to the two charts (pages 12, 13) that you have partially filled in. You will now continue to work with what will be Loop #4 in Chart 1, My Roller Coaster of Addiction.

Reread Loop #3. There you wrote down ways in which you are afraid that others and God would control or punish you, your fears of what would eventually happen to you. Now add to Loop #3 what follows in terms of what you already wrote in Loops #1, #2, #3. Only this time, add to Loop #3 what you believe will happen to you as you get closer to your goals. To put it in another way, how does the material you placed in Loops #1 and #2, as well as Loop #3, relate to your basic beliefs about whether or not you will be able to reach your goals? What does the information there tell you about how you relate to both setting and achieving your goals? What are your negative beliefs and expectations?

Continuing in My Roller Coaster of Addiction, Loop #4, write down the ways you avoid setting goals and the ways you avoid doing the things that help you attain them and find success in life. In short, write down how you sabotage yourself from achieving what you would like to achieve. What are the blocks you set up? How do you get in your own way and impede progress?

Loop #4 is also the addictive loop of the roller coaster, and it is from the energy contained in this loop that we begin to see the emergence of addictive behavior. Even as you write this material down, there may be the urge to close the book, get up from the table, and run off to do something else. Instead of escaping in this way, consider these questions:

- What is your addiction?
- How do you escape this addiction?
- How do you run away?
- Would you like to turn the television on?
- Would you like to get up and clean the house?
- Would you like to cook?
- Would you like to call a neighbor?
- What are the ways you habitually escape dealing with the material that you now have in front of you in Loops #1-4?

How does this behavior set you up for your addictive escape from yourself? Confront this material, deal with it, perhaps even talk it over with someone. If you found difficulty in doing this exercise, it may be important to ask someone to help you fill in the loops from their observations of you. However, get someone who will help you and not do it for you.

Now turn to Chart 2, My Roller Coaster of Healthy

Coasting. In Loop #3, you began to deal with positive beliefs about yourself and others; you listed ways people could begin to see you positively. You may now return to that loop and expand what you have written there. Because you have changed your behavior as cited in Loop #2, and have begun to believe more deeply in yourself and consequently, in Loop #3, believe that people will see you in a more positive way, continue to write how it will be possible for you to set and achieve goals. Write the logical and positive outcomes that would result from acting and behaving as you have reconstructed them in Loops #2, 3.

Now, rather than escaping the goals you are to set for yourself, use Loop #4 to write down what your goals are. Write down how you believe God wants you to attain your goals, how God is on your side in this. You can begin there and continue on another piece of paper. This may take some time but write in that loop the positive things you believe can happen to you if you believe in yourself and in the positive behavior you have described in the loops of My Roller Coaster of Healthy Coasting.

Set a six-month goal for yourself. You might even set more than one goal. Also set a one-year goal, a two-year goal, and then, list a five-, a ten-, and a twenty-year goal for your life. Do some very positive planning. If you have difficulty setting goals and feel that you still don't know yourself well enough to do so, it may be important to consult a career counseling center or guidance center that can help you get in touch with the nature of the person you are and to help you set some positive goals for reaching what ultimately will give you satisfaction.

Repeating It 20 Times
I will set goals for my life and allow myself to achieve them.

Reflecting on Scripture
Ephesians 6:10–17
There is probably no finer set of life goals that those listed in this reading. This Scripture is particularly strong because St.

Paul sees setting goals, life goals, as a way of winning the spiritual war against evil. How wise he is. A lack of goals leaves room for the evil that robs us of the fullness of life that God has intended for us.

Praying

Lord, it is difficult for me to believe that I can set goals and achieve them. Help me to believe that you have given me the power necessary to be able to set and achieve my goals, even in the face of difficulty that sometimes seems even evil. Help me, I pray, to believe that along with the ability you have bestowed on me you will give me the strength to accomplish the goals I set for my life.

Give me the courage to set goals, even if I am not sure that they are really correct or true for me. Help me to believe they are changeable. Help me to believe, Lord, that I can move forward in attempting to achieve the goals I have set, can risk failing, and in both succeeding and failing set new goals that will bring me closer and closer to you and to being the person you created me to be. Help me, I pray, to run the race of being faithful to the self you have created and to know that, to do so, is to return to you the greatest glory. Amen.

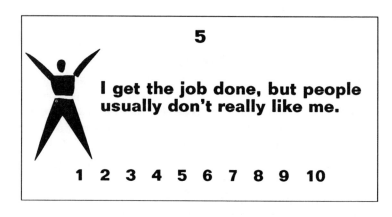

5

I get the job done, but people usually don't really like me.

1 2 3 4 5 6 7 8 9 10

Insight

Our society prizes productivity and achievement. We live in a world where getting a job done is very important. Some would even say, you are what you produce. While that is a very limiting idea of the person, there is a good deal of truth in that what we produce is a reflection of who we are. If getting the job done is so appealing and important, it seems puzzling that many efficient people who are able to get a project completed well and on schedule often have doubts, because of that, about whether or not people really like them. Some of the most successful and accomplished people walk around filled with self-doubt, even though they are really liked, enjoyed, or appreciated by others.

Actually, this phenomenon is not so puzzling. Very often for the accomplished, the achiever, the swing back is to doubt themselves in terms of wondering about whether or not people like them. What makes this often more difficult is that there are times when people don't like achievers because they are threatened by the achiever's ability or cannot handle their success. There are even ideas regarding spirituality that ambition is too close to pride and the accomplishing is seen as less than meek. This reveals an extremely limited, fundamentalist spiritual understanding of our relationship to God.

The Cost of Job Efficiency

Let's deal first with people who do not like you because you are good at getting the job done. If you are going to be efficient, make progress, and be decisive, you are going to upset some people. The more you are in a decision-making position, the greater the possibility that others will not like you. The more you have to decrease options in order to get something accomplished, the less others will like you; they will perceive you as having reduced their freedom. Your effectiveness has a price to pay. If you are effective and get the job done and are generally right, not everyone is going to like you.

There may be some things that you could do to change some of this, but you can never correct the problem entirely. People are all different, and if you are bothered by people liking you because of your efficiency, then be bothered and get it over with; set it aside because it is the reality you have to face.

The people who genuinely do not like you or the way you lead give you important indications about who you may or may not want to work with. The next time you take on a job, you may not want to choose people who do not like to work with you. Or you may decide, even though they don't like you or your style, that these people are important and effective members of the team and you may want to tolerate their dislike of you in order to get the job done. Make your decisions and realize that a part of the fallout is that some are not going to be happy with what you achieve or how you achieve it. Just telling yourself this and giving yourself permission not to be liked or appreciated by everyone can give you a good deal of freedom. This does not mean that you may not have to alter elements of your style, but we will come to that later.

Feeling Guilty about Achieving

More often than not, the sense that people do not like you because you get the job done right and on time emerges from your own negative self-image and from your own guilt over being an achieving, active person. However, feeling that people do not like you can come from making a significant mistake in your thinking, in the way you interpret what people say about your style and what they really think about you. Just because there are negative aspects to the way you get a job done and just because you can rub people the wrong way does not mean that they do not like you. Often, people gripe about managers and leaders and will even mimic and make fun of their behavior. However, these same people actually like effective and achieving supervisors. They may not like the way you have achieved the results, but this does not mean that they do not like you as a person, or accept you. God has created and gifted you and that includes the gifts of administration. Celebrate these gifts.

Co-workers give you a lot more leeway than you think, especially if you are effective. They would rather be on a winning, achieving team than on one that fails. No matter how much they may complain or give you the impression that they don't like you, quite the opposite is likely true.

The plain fact is that people like to complain, and they especially like to complain about someone they believe will not be hurt or upset. If people follow you and help you get the job done, assume that they like you—because that is probably the case. Even though people like to complain, few stop long enough to think that those who lead them also need their support and care. It never occurs to them, but that does not mean that they don't like you.

Moving Into Action

Whenever you find yourself negatively thinking that others do not like you because you are able to get a job completed, stop the thought and correct it by saying, "People like to follow winners" and "Most people like the winners they follow." You may have another way of stopping the negative thought. The important thing is to use it when you are thinking negatively about yourself because you perceive that people don't like you when you are successful.

Exercises in Cooperation

Cooperation and compromise are important in getting things

done. In our age, teamwork and team exercises are becoming increasingly important styles of management. But this leaves out an important factor in leadership: Even in cooperation and compromise, there must be a leader, someone finally responsible for the decisions that are made. You can do all the cooperating and compromising you want, but if you are unable to make big decisions, stick with them, and carry them out, you will fail in accomplishing your goal. Some of the important things you can do in this regard are explained here, ways of enhancing a sense of cooperation and compromise.

Explain Your Style
If you are a supervisor, chairperson, "the boss," it is important at the start of a job to explain your style as you perceive it. Tell people what you like and don't like in getting a job done, and tell them what your style is as you work. Explain how you make decisions and how you include them, your co-workers, in that decision-making process. All this says to them that you are aware of your own style and able to articulate it. Don't be reticent in expressing your style.

If you are an aggressive overachiever, say so. It will be easier for people to accept you if you are honest with them from the beginning. If you tend to be stubborn, say so. If it takes you a while to hear what people really say, let them know that is the case. If you tend to listen and to give in to others too quickly and then to renege, tell people that is a problem that you have in management.

If you are going to lead, don't be ashamed of your style or of expressing it. You will then give people the option of staying on or going their own way. At least no one will be able to say they were surprised at how you get the job done.

Working Styles
An important question to ask those that are going to work with you is, How do you like to work? Simply asking the question indicates a sensitivity to other people's working styles. It also gives you information that may facilitate your decision making down the line. It also provides an opportunity to ex-

press any disagreement with what they tell you about how they work. If, for example, your work day begins at 8:30 and a worker admits that she tends to come in later than that because she is a night person, this might influence whether you wish to work with her.

Whenever possible, try to accommodate the working style of others because it is unlikely that they will change or adjust their working style over a period of time. As long as the overall efficiency of the team is not impeded, accommodate the individual working styles of people who want to be part of a collaborative venture. Such accommodation can make workers content and more effective and thus enhance the prospects of getting the job done. It gives more room for God's grace, which builds upon nature, to work.

Decision Making

How do you make decisions? It is important to communicate what your decision-making style is. If you are not sure of the way you arrive at decisions, do some reading and learn the different styles of coming to a decision. This area is far too broad to handle here, but it is important to know what kind of a decision maker you are if you are going to lead other people and feel comfortable after you have reached your goal.

A leader can't do everything that everyone wants in the way they want it. Decisions have to be made; options have to be refined and narrowed. One of the most important considerations in decision making is to give workers a sense of participation. Whether they have actually affected a decision is not so important as whether they have a sense of having participated in the decision-making process in some way.

Research continues to indicate that those who believe that they have been heard find accepting a decision other than what they would have preferred much easier to accept. A sense of participation in decision making is accomplished by making people feel that you have heard their thoughts, that you have made an effort to elicit feedback in a variety of ways to learn what they think. This goes beyond the suggestion box. It means hearing them out at a particular time in the decision-making process before decisions have been finalized.

Early on in the process, create a sense that everyone can express their ideas without criticism or condemnation. Allow them to talk as long as possible. This kind of idea sharing cannot go on indefinitely, but you will be surprised at how quickly such an open session comes to an end. After a certain time, group members will give those who have too much to say the signal that time is running out. The main thing is to give everyone a sense that they have participated in the ongoing process of what the final outcome will be.

The Roller Coaster of Addiction

The first five Inventory items in this book help you construct the two roller coasters. This Inventory item is the last of the exercises. It concerns the material that will go in Loop #5 and #6 of My Roller Coaster of Addiction, page 12. It is important to have done the exercises of the preceding Inventory items first.

First review the directions for Loop #4 in Chapter 4 before proceeding with the directions here for Loop #5. Turn to pages 34-36 to review this material.

That was what you did for Loop #4 of Chart 1 and Chart 2. Based upon what you wrote there, we now turn to Loop #5 of Chart 1, Defeat.

Write down how you believe you will ultimately fail or how things will fall apart for you, following the progression of what you listed for the previous loops. This, in fact, may already have happened. How have things collapsed around you? If you have recovered and put your life back together, you may want to go on to Loop #6, Compromise, and write down how you have put your life back together but have compromised with life. Write down how you are just reacting, rather than being proactive.

After you have completed Loop #5 on My Roller Coaster of Addiction, turn to Chart 2, My Roller Coaster of Healthy Coasting. In Loop #4 you listed goals. Now list here positive expectations that come from those goals. Perhaps you have already seen some of them become reality. As a result of the different behaviors and expectations you wrote in the previous loops, what logically follows for this loop?

In Loop #5, write down your positive expectations, the good things you believe will happen to you. Be specific and spend some time doing this. It will set you up for success. Loop #6 of Chart 2 naturally follows. It is the joy loop. Joy is the self-fulfilling result of this process. You can write your joys in this box as you discover them through reading this book and doing the exercises.

At this point you might think that there is nothing to put into this box and that's all right. As you do the exercises, pray, and open yourself to God's grace, you will find your self-esteem and your joy increasing.

When you get the job done, doing what you have to do and living your life as an expression of the person you really are, what success can you expect that will enhance and make this cycle stronger and more likely to be repeated?

Repeating It 20 Times
When I get the job done, most people are going to respect and like me. People like to like those who are effective.

Reflecting on Scripture
Hebrews 11:1
This reading tells us that only faith guarantees what we hope for; it is, as we read here, the "assurance of things hoped for." This is the faith it takes to undo the kind of thinking this chapter discusses. It will take faith that the job will get done in the first place, but it will take you even more faith on your part to turn around a negative, self-fulfilling prophecy: that people won't like you when the job does get done. Positive faith turns the habits of negative thinking around; you will need the positive faith described in Hebrews to turn this one around.

Praying
Lord, you got the job done, but not everyone liked you. Those who followed you were those who wanted to walk in truth. Let me see the truth. Let me not believe

that simply because I am ambitious or effective that people who follow the truth will not really like me. Even if
some people don't, let me continue to work toward the
realization of your reign. Amen.

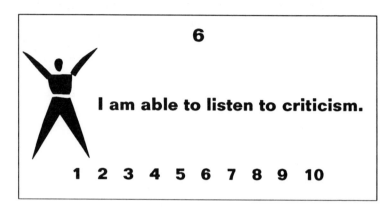

6

I am able to listen to criticism.

1 2 3 4 5 6 7 8 9 10

Insight

The biggest obstacle to accepting criticism is the tendency to take it personally, to interpret the criticism as a putdown of yourself as a person. You think—incorrectly—that the one criticizing you is in fact rejecting you. This undermines self-esteem and keeps you from experiencing yourself as a creation of God. If he or she is rejecting you by the criticism, let the criticism and its motivation be *the other person's problem*.

However, in most cases, criticism is not given as a rejection of the person. Usually when a person cannot take criticism, it is because of the next thing they mentally tell themselves after they hear the criticism. Someone tells you, for example, that they don't like the color you are wearing or the style of your hair. Your next thought is, "This person doesn't like me." Not so. They have simply said they don't like your coat or your hair. You are free to agree or disagree, to care or not care. If the criticism was intended as a way of rejecting you as a person, pay no heed. Such an act is not your problem and is usually not worth bothering with.

Where to Stop

Take another example: Your boss tells you that he doesn't like the way you answer the phone and asks you to change your tone or perhaps even your telephone manner. The negative thought you might have is that your boss doesn't like you or that he is trying to get rid of you. Usually one negative thought will trigger another and you continue to reason irrationally: "There are probably a lot of other things he doesn't like too; he just tolerates me." None of the negative thoughts are necessarily true, and if they are, you certainly don't think or act upon them until you have the concrete data to prove they are true. All your boss said was that he didn't like the way you answer the phone. *Stop right there and listen.* Get more information about what he doesn't like and about how you might answer the phone in a more acceptable manner. Seek further suggestions and find out exactly what is wrong. Then evaluate whether it is valid criticism, whether you can, want to, or should change.

People who do not take criticism well attach a negative thought to the criticism and end up rejecting themselves, seeing it as a rejection of them personally. Feeling rejected by criticism not only defeats self-esteem but causes you to begin to believe that even God rejects you or is critical of you.

There are certainly people who are going to criticize us for the wrong reasons. Usually they are jealous, insecure, or intimidated. They are usually full of their own negativity and need a place to dump it. A priest once told me that there was a group of women in his parish for whom he never did anything right. They always had something to criticize, always found something wrong. As he told me what they said and how they said it, I told him that, in actuality, he was the one who was always rejecting himself. By his own standard, he believed that he could never do anything right. He was harder on himself than those who were criticizing him.

He looked me in the eye and said, "You know, you're right. I am my own worst enemy. I am never satisfied with myself. If it isn't always just perfect, I never let up on myself." "But," he asked, "what do I do with these people who are always criticizing me?" I responded that they would probably always bother him until he changed his attitude about himself. But I also told him that their criticism was their problem, not something he had to take personally or react to. I explained, though, that it would be difficult because these women would likely "hook him" until he let himself off the hook. I also suggested that the criticism was probably their way of getting his attention, and when they saw that it did not work they would change tactics.

Golden Criticism

Most of the time when people criticize us, it's because they want to help us or to make a situation better. Most of the time criticism is a golden opportunity to get good advice without having to pay for a professional consultant. One time, when Cardinal Krol was asked who his spiritual advisor was, he answered that it was just about everyone in the Archdiocese of Philadelphia. Criticism, if we are willing to investigate and consider what is really being said, can be a very good opportunity to find better ways of saying and doing things. It can be a guide to moving in directions that will give our lives more fulfillment and satisfaction. This does not mean that we take every criticism at face value. We weigh criticism; we look into it more. We want it to be as precise and defined as possible.

There are times when criticism is not precise and we only pick up vague indications of something wrong. By beginning to listen and to attune ourselves to receiving more information, problems can be recognized and dealt with before they become larger.

The Defender

People who work in an area called change-agent skills, or the art of creating change smoothly, have learned to identify what they call a defender. This is a person who has much to say that may not always make sense or be on target. However, that person is seen as the voice of many others who remain silent, who will not voice their concern, but will resist change. So the good change-agent will draw out of the defender as many of the concerns as possible to see what truths they might lead to. The defender's statements cannot be accepted at face value, but they may express a deeper discontent, which left unrecognized slows or defeats the process of change.

Moving Into Action

Write down the last three criticisms you received.

What do you believe was their intent?

Should you have sought more information? Did you?

Did you take the criticism personally and feel hurt, or did you listen and deal with what was said?

How much information do you really go after when you are criticized?

From whom do you find it most difficult to receive criticism? Why do you think that this is the case?

Do you need to talk this area of your life over with someone who can hear you out and perhaps offer you some insight?

Repeating It 20 Times

I will not make criticism of me a personal matter, unless it is intended to be. I will see criticism as an opportunity for growth.

Reflecting on Scripture

Sirach 22:27–23:4

These words are an admonition to watch our tongues. Loose talk is of particular concern because the writer is afraid that his errors will multiply and it will be he who ends up looking like a fool because his erroneous ways have not been checked. Criticism is a touchy area and we would be wise to exercise the prudence that the biblical writer suggests.

Praying

Lord, help me to open up and hear criticism without taking it personally. Let me become more aware that you often speak through those around me and that I may not always want to hear what I need to hear. I need to know deep down that you do not reject me. Forgive me for the ways I reject myself and lower my self-esteem and make it seem as though you and others are rejecting me when criticism comes my way. I am often so hard on myself that I find it impossible to believe you love me. Open my ears, Lord, and let me hear; open my heart and enable me to let you love me. Amen.

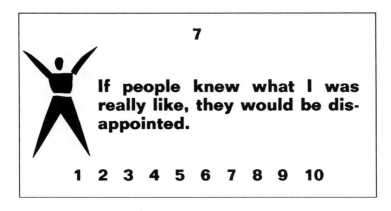

7

If people knew what I was really like, they would be disappointed.

1 2 3 4 5 6 7 8 9 10

Insight

A beautiful plant in my den—lush green leaves and a trail of delicate blossoms—has another part, unseen: a root system, an unattractive tangle of roots in a mess of soil and vermiculite. To a horticulturist, though, the root system would be beautiful: an intricate spread of life-sustaining roots, essential for the growth and beauty of the plant.

In the human personality, what cannot be seen is something like that root system. As human beings, we have some roots that we would just as soon not have the whole world see or know about. Instead of appreciating the lush foliage and blossoms of another person, we, along with the media looking for today's scoop, wonder about the root system. Is he really what he seems to be? For all her beauty, what is she really like? What lies beneath the surface?

If those questions are applied to others, you also apply them to yourself. What would people say if they knew the real me, roots and all?

Feeling Like a Hypocrite

Everyone has some dirty roots. In fact, the word "humility" does not mean some kind of false weakness. Humility comes, as we saw earlier, from the word *humus* and means "dirt."

Humility is truth. And it is not necessary for everyone to know your dirt in order for you to feel pride and accomplishment in your own "lush foliage" and "blossoms"—whatever that might be for you.

It is here that you can get yourself into a terrible bind. Whenever life is going well or whenever others are thinking positively about you, a voice whispers in your mind, "If they only knew what I'm really like." The truth is that if we knew more about what our heroes and our saints were really like, accepting and tolerant people, we would have a lot more heroes and saints including, perhaps, ourselves. It is not necessary for everyone to know your "dirt" for you to feel consistent and whole about yourself. For one thing, it is not their business.

Because there are also things that are bad about you, don't fall into the trap of failing to claim for yourself what is good, your "blossoms." This is a key area for self-esteem. Actually, the things that make you feel most unholy and most unworthy are the very things that can be the source of understanding and accepting others. It is often what we feel most guilty about that draws us to our religions and to our spiritualities. It is what God uses to get you on the road to self-esteem, while evil is whispering in your ear that you are undeserving and unworthy. Nonsense!

If people knew what you were really like, they would probably be relieved that you are human, too. And if they could not accept you, you might want to consider the quality of their friendship. However, don't put everyone to the test.

Moving Into Action

Make a list of all the things about yourself that make you feel unworthy and insignificant. Write down all the "dirt," all of the things that you feel would disappoint others if they knew this about you. Ask yourself how all of these events and realities have been a part of what has added up to make you who you are. In the cases where there is failure, ask yourself what you have learned or realized. How has all of this made you more compassionate and understanding of others?

At some point, share all of this "dirt" with someone you trust. This might be with a priest in the context of the sacrament of reconciliation. It might be with a counselor or with a friend you can trust with confidentiality.

Acceptance

Make a decision to begin accepting yourself. Rather than rejecting all the negative things about yourself, enter into a process of acceptance. This does not mean that you accept or give in to negative behavior as if it didn't matter how you lived. Perhaps there will be areas where you need to reach out for help and healing. Often, the areas that cannot be accepted are the ones that continue to have the greatest hold on you.

If you are a religious person, decide to give everything you listed as an offering to God. Offer to God this negative side of you, your dirty roots, and ask God to use them in a redemptive and restorative way. You might want to do this physically. Go to a church and place on the altar this list of negative things. Actually offer it there. Then take the list home and burn it as a symbol of being consumed in the love God has for you.

When you begin to think that if people knew you they wouldn't accept you, stop that negative pattern of thought right there and then. Recognize that you are thinking negatively and repeat the brief statement below over and over. If the negative thinking continues, reread this item and perhaps even do the exercise of listing and offering. Whatever you do, don't give in to the little voice that wants to convince you that you are a hypocrite. If you become convinced that you are, you will blossom less and less and give less of what only you can give to the world.

Repeating It 20 Times

Humility is truth. I am who I am, and even my mistakes have helped me to become the person I am. My faults do not make my "blossoms" less real.

Reflecting on Scripture

Romans 5:1–11

A quote from St. Thérèse of Liseux goes something like this: "God does not punish us for being bad nor reward us for being good, but asks from us patience while he does his work of holiness in us." The assuring scripture from Romans is similar. It reminds us that there is nothing we can do for our sinful state that Christ has not already done in his sacrifice on the cross. What is required of us, a gift from God, is our faith that Christ has reconciled us, roots and dirt, that we are made whole in God's sight, and that God's love has been poured into our hearts.

Praying

Lord, I sometimes think that it is you accusing me when I feel hypocritical and inconsistent. I sometimes believe that you are the one that is whispering in my ear and telling me that I am not worthy and undeserving of love and good things. Lord, I have often blamed you for making me feel like I should be disappointed in myself.

Help me, I pray, to realize that you desire me to believe in myself and to be proud of the "blossoms" in my life. Help me to believe that when I once take my "dirt" to you in repentance, it becomes a matter of the past, forgotten. Break the patterns of my self-inflicted sense of hypocrisy and let me go free to extend your love into the world. Thank you, Lord. Amen.

8

Every once in a while I have to do something to let people know that I am not really "holy."

1   2   3   4   5   6   7   8   9   10

Insight

If, in fact, you do have to do something every once in a while to show others that you are not so holy, why are you trying to be so holy? If you answer that you are not trying to be holy, then why do others see you in this light?

It may well be that you are in a position in which the expectations that others have of you seem overly demanding. You may find yourself in a position where people expect a standard of behavior associated with a particular standing or profession in life. The problem, though, is not their expectations of good and righteous behavior on your part. Their expectations will change. If you feel the necessity to show them you aren't holy, you are already caught up in their expectations. But their expectations are only that. They have many ways, direct and indirect, of communicating to you when you are not fulfilling them.

However, the expectations you are reacting to are not those of others, but your own. You are, in reality, showing yourself that you aren't holy, reacting against your expectations of yourself. Those who place their expectations on you and whom you must occasionally convince of your "unholiness" are really an extension of yourself. Your own high standards of self-esteem leave you feeling as though you can't measure up to your inner ideal, that you can't be holy enough, and your self-esteem is lowered. You can also begin to believe that you don't measure up to God's expectations. You who have put yourself in the "holy" category must now and then break out of it. You have constrained yourself by your own expectations.

When you are comfortable with your expectations of yourself, with your behavior, you will not feel constrained by others' expectations of you.

People may have a need to see you as "holy." And you may very well need to allow them to see you that way. They—and you—must also accept the fact that they may from time to time be disappointed. It is your responsibility to be who you are and to realize that when you must convince others that you are not holy you are really trying to convince yourself and to give yourself the room to be who you are. No one's expectations can box you in unless you allow it. The only time the expectations of others can confine us is when we have the same unrealistic, subconscious expectations of ourselves.

Don't be afraid to be someone else's hero. Don't be afraid to let someone admire you for fear that they may find out that you are human. People need heroes; they need people to admire. You can be one of them. If we are going to wait for perfect heroes and entirely consistent people to come along, we will wait a long time. It's all right for you to be a role model and be imperfect at it. People have a way of seeing what they want to see and discounting what doesn't go along with their pre-existing ideas and images. You don't have to get caught up in that, unless you have the need to see yourself as something "other" or "more than" you are.

Moving Into Action

Don't be so hard on yourself. You probably aren't fooling anyone anyway—unless they want to be fooled. Lighten up.

Repeating It 20 Times

Humility is truth. I am most holy when I am the self God

created me to be. I can be comfortable with and esteem who I am, even though I am incomplete and always growing.

Reflecting on Scripture

Psalm 42:9–12

The psalmist cries out to his downcast soul and proclaims that God is the rock and the true holy one. The scripture tells the one who is being very hard on self to lighten up and place hope in God. Sometimes we can become so downcast because of the expectations we believe others have of us but which have been placed there by ourselves. The scripture calls us to put our hope in God, not in our own ability to make ourselves holy. The enemy who oppresses, according to this psalm, is none other than ourselves.

Praying

Lord, just as the psalmist says, you give me your grace one day at a time. Forgive me when I allow the expectations of others to interfere with my own expectations of myself. Help me to realize that I am often my own oppressor when I expect of myself behavior that is not a true reflection of who I am. I blame others for oppressing me with unrealistic expectations, yet, at heart, I am the real culprit. If I did not do the same to myself, I wouldn't even listen to them.

You are my "rock," Lord. It is not you who have forgotten me; it is I who forgot myself, who forgot to be the person you created me to be. When I am downcast, help me to first look at myself and the pressure I am putting on myself. Help me when I am doing something to convince others I am not really holy. Make me ask myself what I am really doing.

Lord, I am the song you want to sing. Never let me try to be someone else's song. Amen.

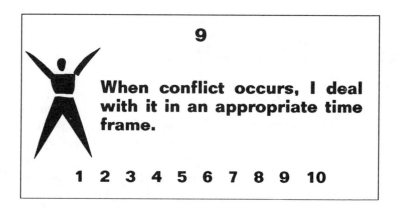

9

When conflict occurs, I deal with it in an appropriate time frame.

1   2   3   4   5   6   7   8   9   10

Insight

Not all conflict can or should be dealt with on the spot. Some conflict is better left alone for a while so there can be a "cooling off" period; other kinds of conflict need to be dealt with at the time so that the matter goes no further. People have two modes in which they deal with conflict, passively or actively, and all of us swing somewhere along that continuum.

Passive Mode

At one extreme, passive people tend to bury conflict and hope it will go away, undermining self-esteem. Conflict is never faced and becomes internalized; it is kept tucked away inside. Confrontation is thus avoided and seldom is a conflict resolved. Sometimes this can work, though. If the conflict has not been major, people do tend to forgive and forget and to get on with the business of living. They go on as if nothing happened. There are situations, as you may know from experience, in which it is better if the whole issue is just dropped. Let it be and recognize that people do have differences. Often, we have to tell children to just "drop it," to "forget it" and to go on with their business, and sometimes we have to tell ourselves and other adults the same thing. "Dropping the matter" and "forgetting it" can provide an appropriate response to dealing with conflict. God will also grace us to forget. There are certainly instances where this is good advice.

This mode avoids the cycle of frustration and anger. Once involved in conflict, you may find that you simply carry it on and on as it eats at you, and that the more you talk about the conflict and work on it, the more involved, upset, and driven you become. It may seem that you can't let it go. Being able to put it behind you and walk away can be a healthy solution in such instances.

Passive people are well aware that time does heal some wounds. That the passage of time itself takes away the intensity of the moment allows time for feelings to discharge and subside, and more rational thinking can take place. People can change the way they feel about a particular situation because they have had time to change the way they think about it.

"Time out" is an important behavioral exercise many teachers and therapists use in a situation where "cooling off" and distance give emotionally involved people a chance to exercise cognitive control, that is, put their calm, objective thinking into action. The decision not to deal with conflict *at the time* is a plausible decision and can be a very wise one.

It is good not to take action immediately in a conflict situation, to take your time dealing with it. However, it is important to realize that "no action" is, in itself, action. There can be as much energy involved in taking "no action" as there is in acting upon a situation. This is why the word "passive" is a kind of misnomer. While it may define a style of handling conflict, the word suggests that nothing is happening. In holding a situation in "unresolve," even more energy may be involved because the conflict is left in "limbo." Passivity is never really an escape from conflict; it is merely a different way of dealing with it.

Passivity Can Backfire
Here is an important consideration in deciding how to deal with conflict. You may have learned that things "cool off"

when conflict is not handled immediately and you may have judged that this is an easier solution to all conflict. Because some situations have worked out better by not jumping in and getting matters reconciled right away, you may have developed a style of handling all your conflicts in this manner. What you need to realize is that usually the same amount of emotional and psychic energy is involved in handling conflict in a passive or in an active manner. The main consideration in making this decision is what produces the greatest gain for everyone concerned and provides the best solution.

If you stick your head in the sand in the face of conflict and hope that it will always work itself out in time, you are also stuffing your emotions and your mind with energy that works against you, negative energy. Stuffing conflict, ignoring it in the hope that it will go away of itself, causes avoidance behavior, creates a sense of uncertainty and a lack of confidence. It allows anxiety to build and fearfulness to develop. The refusal to deal with conflict eventually expresses itself in subtle and more pronounced forms of hostility: expressions and actions which, while not directly expressing anger, do express displeasure and discontent. Energy that is internalized will always find a way out in the form of anxiety, obsessive-compulsive behavior, and addictive styles of behavior. Some people actually exhibit very low levels of energy because so much of it is used up in keeping conflict inside.

Active Mode
For all of the wisdom and control there may be in taking "time out," a period to cool off, that mode may not always be possible. As much as we might want to drop something and forget it and get on with business as usual, that will not always work in the short term or in the long run. In fact, it can even cause more difficulty. Oftentimes, not dealing with conflict does not allow important information that should come out "at the time" to make itself known, and this information later becomes obscure and forgotten and impedes the resolution. Unresolved conflict can cause distancing behavior and things simply don't get done. The interests of the good of peo-

ple and projects fade and enthusiasm and productivity are lost.

Actively dealing with conflict means facing up to the situation, getting the facts together, and doing what you have to do. This will lead to resolving issues, arriving at a reconciliation, and getting things over with so they do not have time to fester and cause even more problems.

Actively dealing with conflict means that you and the other party have to face each other and try to communicate your differences. It may mean that you have to deal with a conflict inside yourself first, a conflict you need to resolve, a decision that you need to bring to light so that you can be clear about what you are going to do in the conflict. Bring your conflict to a satisfactory conclusion; getting it done and over with can give you a new sense of freedom and more energy for the rest of your day-to-day life.

Most conflicts don't go away. When it is not brought into the open soon, the details of a situation become vague, leaving room for rumors and suspicion that create even more uncertainty. We can become uncertain and out of touch with ourselves and where we really stand in a situation. By avoiding dealing with what must be handled eventually, we can lose track of where reality is in a given situation, even when the conflict exists inside. This does not mean that a conflict can be resolved all at once. Some conflicts require time to resolve, and time to heal the pain that may accompany it.

It is generally best to deal with conflict in an active mode because it saves energy and confusion. However, what is important with regard to self-esteem is that you are not stuck in a single mode of handling it. Passive people who are inclined to deal with conflict only in a passive manner tend to lack the self-confidence and the practical skills to get the matter resolved. Active people tend to express their insecurity by dealing with every conflict as though it were the same and to be handled in the same immediate manner. "Getting it over with" expresses a lack of confidence in handling difficult emotions over a period of time. Not dealing with conflict, again, undermines self-esteem.

A Rule of Thumb

A general rule of thumb is to deal with conflict as soon as possible except in situations that are so emotionally charged that time is needed to allow the parties to think through the alternatives. Sometimes conflict may be resolved only over a long period of time and gentleness must be the rule. God will give us the wisdom and patience to deal with conflict.

Again, what is important is the range of your repertoire in dealing with conflict. How flexible are you in this regard? Do you deal with it in a manner that is appropriate to the nature of the conflict and in a suitable time frame, or are you stuck in either the passive or active mode of dealing with it?

A good self-image and good self-esteem mean that you have enough confidence in yourself to handle a variety of ways of dealing with conflict, and that you are able to assess the situation and others' needs and fears as well as your own.

Moving Into Action

Make a chart labeled "Handling Conflicts." In the first column, list the conflicts. See if you can find three conflicts that involve others and two conflicts within yourself. In a second column, write down how you are presently dealing with the conflict. In a third column, write down how you would deal with the conflict in an active, "take the bull by the horns," mode. In a fourth column, write down how you would deal with the conflict in a passive, "let it sit for a while," mode. Then make some decisions about the best way of dealing with each of the conflicts. In a fifth column, give yourself a deadline for dealing with each of these situations.

Repeating It 20 Times

There are many ways of dealing with conflict and I can handle them. I can be effective in dealing with conflict and I am here and now deciding to do so, with God's help.

Reflecting on Scripture

Matthew 6:9–13

In the Lord's Prayer we ask that our trespasses be forgiven, and we also say that we forgive the trespasses, the sins and offenses, of others. However, this doesn't mean that Christians won't have to deal with conflict. It is a doormat spirituality that does not deal with conflict in such a way that Christian growth can occur. For growth there must be conflict; it's a part of life. However, the Lord's Prayer also tells us that we will be given our "daily bread," the strength and wisdom we need, to deal with conflict.

Praying

Lord, I'd rather not face conflict. I'd like to pretend that it will go away. It isn't easy to express disagreement and displeasure or to hear this in others. It's easier to hope that these unpleasant matters will just take care of themselves. But I realize that what I do with external conflicts, I also do with interior ones. I don't deal with my own internal conflicts. I don't forgive myself sometimes. I often don't give myself enough "daily bread" of emotional care so that I stay in touch with what is bothering me, which allows me to be the free person you call me to be.

Grant me, Lord, the courage and strength to face conflict and the common sense to use the gifts you have already given me to be more gentle and more active in resolving my own inner conflicts. Amen.

10

I can be stubborn.

1 2 3 4 5 6 7 8 9 10

Insight

The difference between stubbornness and perseverance is one of dependency. Believe it or not, stubborn people are insecure and want to remain dependent upon things the way they know them, on their own terms. They are fearful of encountering other ways of seeing and doing things that threaten their self-defined sense of security.

Stubbornness is a way of controlling other people, which usually begins in childhood. The child learns that by holding out and by being non-compliant that others will eventually give in. The child, at an early age, has learned that he or she can remain dependent upon the environment by controlling others through sheer willfulness.

Stubborn people are fearful people in the disguise of stubbornness.

If you know that you are stubborn and you scored yourself high on this Inventory item, it is important to ask yourself if your stubbornness really gets you what you want, or if it does not, does it keep you tied to others or to a structure that is basically unsatisfying? The problem is that you are afraid to risk finding more of your own way in life. In making unrealistic demands upon those around you, the false security you provide yourself only traps you further in what never satisfies your needs. As a result, you become even more stubborn, even though you may appear to others as "determined." Plain and simple, stubbornness is a mark of insecurity and impedes your growth into mature adulthood.

Often young people who keep returning home, unable to stabilize themselves in the world "out there," are basically too stubborn to enter into the give-and-take that is demanded of maturity. They return home where their stubbornness will be tolerated only because home is the one place that cannot turn them away. Stubbornness also undermines our spiritual growth and we remain dependent on God as we have "created" God to be for us. Because of a lack of growth, self-esteem cannot emerge.

There can be a similar problem for members of religious and academic institutions. People often use religious professions and the traditional vows of poverty, chastity, and obedience, which are misunderstood, to insure a structure of dependency where they can remain basically selfish and not have to grow. In academic institutions, there is more than one professor who has used the often ill-defined and ambivalent authority of the academic institution to insure a position where stubbornness can be exercised. People behave themselves long enough to find their niche, and when firmly entrenched, begin to exercise the stubbornness that affects others and the productivity of the system. The problem is also found in the general workplace where insecure managers will not confront stubborn people with the reality that other needs beyond their own, especially the well-being of the company, must be ensured.

If you are a stubborn person, it is vital to understand that you express your insecurity in your stubbornness, and you ensure dependence upon a structure or a set of relationships that keep you from growing into the fullness of the person you are.

Moving Into Action
List for yourself some areas in which you are stubborn, so that you can see in front of you exactly how you are stubborn. What is your "stubborn style"?

Ask yourself how being stubborn keeps you dependent upon others or upon structures that are not satisfying for you. Write out your response.

Ask yourself how you first learned to be stubborn. Who would respond? How would they respond? How did you feel afterwards? Write out your response.

If being stubborn is a real problem for you, you may want to talk with someone about it. If you are so stubborn that you feel you are losing a really important part of yourself, get professional counseling. Seek to understand more about the roots of your insecurity. As you gain understanding, don't expect understanding alone to change you. You must, with insight, decide how to behave differently and do it.

Repeating It 20 Times
I can get my needs met in honest and open ways. I can give up stubbornness as a way of controlling.

Reflecting on Scripture
Psalm 95

In this psalm, we read of joyfully praising Yahweh and of recognizing that it is God who is God and not us. Although a psalm of thanksgiving, it is also a reminder of our place in relationship to God. The psalm goes on to entreat us to prostrate ourselves in humility before Yahweh. We are called to listen, actually warned to listen, rather than to harden our hearts. The psalm reminds a stubborn people that God is God and that it is God's ways that are important to hear, learn, and respect. It also reminds us that when things do not go our way, stubbornness can be a response of pride that allows us to play God rather than to open ourselves to the wonderful and awesome working of God. It is true that eventually even the most impossible situations work out with faith in God, even if it isn't how we imagine it would be. Becoming stubborn just slows down our growth process and wastes our energy needlessly.

Praying

Lord, show me where I am stubborn and how my stubbornness works against me. I want to be determined and persevering, but I don't want to control people in ways that harm me and my relationship with them. Give me the courage to believe that you have given me the gifts to make things happen positively, without relying on stubbornness.

Help me, Lord, to look more deeply at what is "my way" and to discover whether I'm really in touch with what will give my life meaning and purpose. Am I trying to hold on to something that must go if I am to grow and become happier with others and myself? Grace me with your guiding Spirit. Amen.

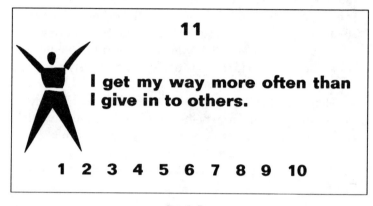

11

I get my way more often than I give in to others.

1 2 3 4 5 6 7 8 9 10

Insight

The issue in this Inventory item is not whether you can get your own way; it is whether or not you can give in to others and how you feel when you do. It's true that there are people who are always giving in to others as a way of remaining dependent and not having to grow, but that isn't the issue here. Anyone with the sense that they can get their way more than they give in either has an inflated sense of their power or is exercising too much power inappropriately. Having always to "get one's way" is a mark of insecurity. Whether we like it or not, we are simply too interconnected with others to think that "our way" is really ours alone and not the result of many who enable us and are a part of our world.

If you get your way more than you give in, someone is supporting you, enabling you to do this. In some way, you have constructed your world, used your position of power or someone's need to be dependent to insure getting your own way.

But the plain fact is that getting your way in this world is not nearly so important as having the skills to be able to give in. If you think about it for a moment, you will realize something that good business people have always known: By "giving in" most of the time, you create a system where you get your way when it is really important to do so. People who always get their own way end up fighting battles that, in the end, don't really matter so much. They win the battle but lose the war, so to speak.

It is not very often in life that you actually get "your own way." Most of life is filled with the give-and-take of agreements and compromises that make the end result the product of many people's input.

Giving In as a Skill

Giving in has become synonymous with being weak or losing. And yet this is completely irrational when we look at the ways we have to behave most of the time. Very often giving in takes a strength and skills in interpersonal relationships that are much more difficult than "getting your way." People who can give in have learned to let go of the everyday losses of life, and to "go along" with others because they have a sense of the greater good of an overall endeavor. They also have a greater sense of God's plan and God's timing.

Obviously, this does not mean that you "give in" when moral issues are involved or that you give in when to do so would violate the person you are. You don't give in over and over again when it is not good for the other person and allows inappropriate controlling behavior. But here we are not talking about whether or not you can "get your way," whatever that might be; we are talking about whether or not you can give in and not feel "diminished" and "less than."

Giving In

How does it feel when you really give in? Many people think they are giving in, but they are fooling themselves and others. It looks like they are team players. They talk things over with everyone and make them feel that their input is important, but through their methods of control things always end up being done their way.

Giving in really means seeing things from another point of view. It is the essence of any truly artistic and creative endeavor. When an artist creates, in whatever form the creativity takes, the "known" is suspended in favor of the unknown. The artist enters into the experience of the "other" perspective and creates a different way of seeing things. An artist is a sponge for feedback, soaking up data and then suspending knowing and creating something.

People who are good at conflict management, in settling disputes, are artists in finding ways that people can reach agreement by getting them to consider options in a new way. These people create a situation in which "giving in" is easier for each side; they lead both sides to an outcome in which neither side will feel as though the other side "got their way."

Negotiation as Art

The art of negotiating is the art of living, and people who think they are getting their own way are usually poor negotiators. In fact, if you always get your own way, or think you do, your skills of negotiating are probably at a minimum. When was the last time you asked yourself how you could turn a potential situation into a minimum of losses for all parties concerned? When was the last time you thought about strategies that "saved face" for the party in a dispute that might lose what they wanted? These are important questions in a world where people have access to more and more information and have more and more ways of solving problems.

Giving in at the right time and in the right way is an art to be cultivated rather than a burden to be borne. Giving in carries a built-in learning situation. It will help to either confirm or refine your ideas or teach you that there are, in fact, other ways of doing things. There are also going to be times when you wish that you had never given in, but that is also a part of the learning process.

False Independence

It is true that we have to depend upon ourselves and develop the skills of self-reliance so that we don't depend upon others for things we should be doing for ourselves. But for many years, we have promoted a false idea of independence and raised being "independent" as a false standard. Being an independent person isn't all it's cracked up to be. In fact, being independent really isn't much fun. In creating "independent" people we have created lonely and selfish people. Giving in seems like a dirty word to them, as though they have been robbed.

Giving in does not mean being a doormat. Just the opposite; a person makes other people doormats by having to ensure that they get their own way more often than they give in. That just isn't realistic or healthy. I have seen married couples on the verge of divorce because they wouldn't "give a little" and let go of their airtight ideas of what their marriage and their spouse should be like.

Giving in is movement outward from the mind and heart that gives the other person a chance, that allows others to feel more involved, that engages you more in the lives of other people because you really want to learn where they are coming from. Giving in means surrender to God, in a sense, and that surrender, over time, will increase self-esteem.

Moving Into Action

Identify some situations in which you have moderate to strong opinions. Be clear what it is that you want in these instances. Where would it be advisable for you to give in a little?

Where could you give in and in the long run be more effective in your involvement?

Where would giving in increase the participation and the sense of acceptance on the part of another person or persons?

Is it possible in any of these situations for you to do something that enables another person to "save face"?

Can you identify a situation in which another person or persons are destined to be losers and find a way to minimize their losses in some way? This may be in simply making them feel important, significant, or cared about.

As you open your mind to new possibilities in interpersonal relationships, decide to do them. The ancient spiritual discipline can be practiced here. If you give up something for Lent or make a sacrifice during some special religious season, practice detachment not so much from things as from "your way" of seeing and doing things. The greatest act of giving may well be giving in in such a way that others become more a part of, and feel more significantly attached to, your life.

Repeating It 20 Times

Giving in is not a weakness. I can develop this wise and cultured skill.

Reflecting on Scripture

Matthew 5:40–44

In this scripture meditation Christ tells us to turn the other cheek, and if someone asks us for our pants to give them our shirt as well. We are also told to love our enemies and to pray for those who persecute us. Tough sayings! It is often very difficult to go two miles when someone has already asked us to go one mile and we didn't want to do that. Christ speaks strongly to make a point. Christian charity is a primary sign to the world of the life of Christ within us and a primary witness to the power of the Holy Spirit to enable us to do things we didn't want to. Giving in when we want to hold out is very much a part of the love Christ speaks of, especially when we like to have it our way.

Praying

Lord, I am terribly afraid of giving in. It feels like I am no longer in control and that I am losing a part of myself. If I give in, it feels like I won't be able to give myself credit for anything. I am afraid that if I give in, I won't feel significant and important, and others won't admire and like me as much as I would like.

I do know one thing, Lord. I don't really always get my own way, and I confess I don't like it very much when I don't. I can even become spiteful and hope others will fail. Forgive me that all of this seems so important to me and forgive me for what I do to myself by having to be in control. Lord, may I learn, by your grace, to give in and to let others help me and know me as I really am: needy and wanting to be loved, even though I'm afraid of it. Amen.

12

It is difficult for me to ask for help.

1 2 3 4 5 6 7 8 9 10

Insight

A difficulty with asking for help usually begins in childhood. What happened when as a child you asked others for help? Can you remember how teachers or parents responded to your requests? If help was freely and easily given, the practice of asking for it was reinforced and you expected it.

Passivity

Many people can think of instances when they reached out for help and "got their hands slapped" in one way or another. At that point they may have decided that that would be the last time they'd ask for help. From then on, they would get along by themselves. You may have had a similar experience. Asking for help or needing it might mean that you would be rejected or reprimanded. Children often learn not to ask for help in school when teachers tell them: "You don't pay attention." "If you weren't daydreaming, you wouldn't have to ask."

Not asking for help is generally a protection from not wanting to be rejected. You have the irrational belief that people will reject you and let you down. Actually, the opposite is true. People like to say yes to requests for help more than they like to say no.

The "I'd rather do it myself" attitude may seem to come from false pride and stubbornness, but it is really a cover for not wanting to be rejected and let down. The other person may say no, or you fear what they will think of you if they know you need help.

Asking for help is actually a way of sharing with others. One of the most important gifts we can give others is to allow them to give a gift of themselves to us. People need to be needed, and in asking others for help, you invite them to share in your life; you are giving them an opportunity to be a part of it. Asking for help is an opportunity for social interchange, a healthy sign of an ability for give-and-take. "Loners" do not like to ask for help because it may lead to another's intrusion into their lives. You cannot be alone and also ask for help. It is God's design that we seek the assistance of others; that is also an important part of our prayer. Being able to reach out is an important signpost of self-esteem.

Needing to Be Indispensable

A part of the fear of asking for help is the need to be indispensable. There is the story of the highly successful bakery business that had always been kept in the family. The baker, though, kept all of the recipes in his head because he was afraid that if others had them he would not be needed. When he died, his recipes died with him and so did his bakery.

Sometimes people in a work situation make sure that others do not know how to do their jobs when they are away for a time. These people will keep secrets, hide papers, and generally confuse the system by creating a process that is so much their own that no one could possibly take over the job. Eventually this backfires. The person becomes ill or the business grows and others must be included. The one who made himself indispensable is eased out, often before he realizes it. The best way to advance on a job is to learn all you can and to teach others what you know. This builds up trust and shows competence. In the process you inevitably have to ask others for help.

Doing It Yourself

If you want something done "your way," then you may have to do it yourself. If you are poor at communicating what you want or impatient explaining it to others, you may have to do it yourself. If you are unsure about what you want, you may have to do it yourself. But if you tire of doing everything yourself, then you have to grow out of needing to be "indispensable."

Most of the time, when you take over a task that is well defined and explained, you add your own creativity and way of doing things. But if you always have to do things yourself, you either need to be indispensable or you are too controlling. Shared responsibility and shared creativity are always more productive.

Not Wanting to Help

One Christmas, two teenage daughters enjoyed a Christmas dinner their parents had prepared. After the dinner, they announced that they were tired and were going to take a nap. Obviously they didn't want to help with the cleanup and the parents' request for help would be turned down. To the parents, it was not a matter of whether they cared to help or not. To them, it was important to ask, no matter how the daughters might feel about it. When people are selfish and thinking only of themselves, we owe it to their self-image and to ourselves to be assertive enough to ask them for help.

People often need to be taught by being asked to help. The possibility of helping never dawns on some people. They were not taught to see how they can help, and they are so self-absorbed that it simply never occurs to them that, although others are certainly capable of doing something themselves, they should not have to do so.

Don't be afraid to let others know that they ought to help when they have not thought of it. Even when you can do it yourself, don't. You help no one and accomplish little except probably add to your own "doormat" reputation or to your own resentment, or both.

Moving Into Action

Make a list of ten areas in your life where ideally you would need or like to have help. After you have listed them, list them from the most important area to the least important.

Take the list you have drawn up and talk to a friend about how you could get help in the top five areas. If you don't feel comfortable with a friend or family member, seek professional counseling. Make a plan in each of the areas and within one month, implement the plan for the five areas. Make up your mind to ask for help and get working on it.

Repeating It 20 Times

I can ask for help. People want to help me.

Reflecting on Scripture

Psalm 143

This is a magnificent cry for help. It is one of many psalms that teach us that asking for help is important, fundamental to healthy and wholesome living for Christians.

Praying

Give me the courage to ask others to help me and to know that my request may be a gift for them or a time of teaching them something they need to learn. Let me overcome my fear of being rejected.

Since I am not God and only you are God, I need first of all to seek your help in all I do and at every moment of my life. Then I need to ask others, and invite you and them into my life. I don't like to admit that I have needs, Lord, and that I can't do it all by myself. But I can't. You know and I know it, so who am I fooling? And, by your grace, may I always stand ready to assist others. Amen.

13

I tend to be the accommodating person.

1 2 3 4 5 6 7 8 9 10

Insight

Accommodating others can be a sign of hospitality when the accommodation is by choice or without a sense of using the other person. As the word is used and understood here, it refers to a tendency to be too accommodating. People who score high on this Inventory item tend to be overly accommodating, rather than accommodating out of a sense of choice. Their accommodation comes as a result of a sense of obligation and is filled with the shoulds of eventual "hostile hospitality," which is accommodating others because you "should" and not because you freely choose to.

Accommodating others extends beyond the realm of hospitality. It extends into a compulsive area of life, where, if you scored yourself high on this item, you usually "go along" and do what will keep others happy. You are the one who gives in and accommodates the needs and wishes of others. At least, you perceive yourself as doing so.

It is questionable whether persons who perceive themselves as accommodating really are as accommodating as they think they are. Usually there is a "hitch" or a "hook" to their being too accommodating.

If you are overly accommodating, you most likely feel almost compelled to let the other person have her way. If you do not, you feel guilty and feel you have to make it up to her.

What You Want

Accommodating others is often easier than: 1) figuring out what it is you yourself want in the first place, 2) being assertive enough to go after what you want.

One of the objections I usually hear from people who are too accommodating is, "Well, isn't it all right to be a giving person? Is there anything wrong with wanting to make others happy?" No, of course there isn't, but that is usually an excuse for not having a grip on one of the two qualities just mentioned.

First of all, it's important to know what you want before you develop a habit of letting other people define your wants and likes. There is nothing wrong with experiencing what pleases other people; in fact, trying new things and new experiences is very desirable. But relying on other people to define your needs and tastes and to lead you into their activities as an excuse for not coming to grips with your own tastes is destructive. There is no question that we learn who and what we are in relationship with others, with exchanging experiences. But there can be so much experiencing of what others want that there is no real sharing. In other words, both sides have to be giving so that the sum of the two parts can be greater than the whole. You shortchange others when you allow them to define your life. You also shortchange God. The Spirit of God is alive and growing in you, informing you of who you are. Quiet times and listening prayer bring this to the surface. As this sense of God alive in us grows, so does our self-esteem.

Also, other people need to know how to accommodate you in order that they can grow as well; they need to encounter your desires in order to expand their own world. The experience of "you" is as important to others as your experience of them. In the process you learn who you really like to be with and how often you like to be with them.

Many people have entered marriage only to find that during courtship (if there was a real courtship) the person they married had only been saying what he or she thought they wanted to hear. After the wedding, they encounter a person they never knew because he or she was hidden during the "getting to know" period of their relationship.

You have a responsibility to other people to let them know what is important to you, what your tastes and preferences are, and to show them the way you make your demands on life. People you are getting to know have a right to know this about you, and you have an obligation to share yourself not just for your own good, but for theirs as well.

We define our experience with and against the experiences of others, but they also do the same. We need them and they need the "real" us rather than the accommodating person that plays the game only on the other person's terms.

The second area to overcome in being too accommodating is being assertive enough to make the proper demands to obtain what is important to you. You may find that the person you are getting to know or have known can live only according to their perceptions of reality—according to the way they see things—and that they will allow little or no room for you to be who you really are. This calls the nature of your relationship into question. There are ways of controlling another person in such a way that their real needs are never met. If you are not in touch with yourself, accommodating others may result in a mistaken notion of who you really are.

It may also be just what you want to have happen so you don't have to do the work of really coming to grips with the person you are. You may think (and you may be right) that doing so means trouble for you, for someone else, or for both.

Going After What You Want

When you go after what you want and what is important to you, one thing is certain: To some degree you are going to disrupt the lives of those around you, because they are going to have to accommodate you in new and different ways. This is why timing is important in being assertive. If you have spent a lifetime accommodating others, you probably don't want to start being assertive overnight. It will be a process that should be gentle, even though it is sure to rock the boat. Temper what is said here with wisdom and patience.

Most people don't really go after what they want. And even those who do are afraid to change course if they find out later they really want something else. Safety seems to be the norm.

Eventually you will have to go after what is important for you. What you must realize is that in the long run the disruption will probably be as important to others' lives as it is to your own. We are a terribly self-centered generation, so it is difficult to talk about this simply. Many of the "me" generation sought what they thought was important to them, only to find out that they hadn't thought about it well enough and long enough and had not included others in the big picture.

This Inventory item is not for the "me generation"; it is for those who are more accommodating than they ought to be for their own good or for the good of those around them. We do not help others define who they really are and come to know what they can do in the world if we will not do the same for ourselves. Living your life in a way that accommodates primarily the needs of others creates unhealthy dependencies, resentment, and a listlessness and boredom with life, not only for you but in the whole system of which you are a part.

Moving Into Action

Ask yourself the following questions:

• Where do I accommodate others to the extent that I compromise myself?

• Where does my giving in cause another not to grow?

• What does the Spirit of God seem to be doing in me or moving me toward?

If there is someone you have to forgive, make the decision to forgive that person. If possible and appropriate, put the forgiveness in actual motion and let the person know that you forgive him or her. Realize, though, that this may not be appropriate or possible. If you are confused, seek some advice. Let go of your resentment wherever it exists and if you can't, make the decision to begin working toward it, one day at a time.

When you have finished these two assignments, do something very special for yourself. Give yourself a gift. Do something good for yourself and enjoy the experience.

This is not an Inventory item you have to do all in one day. You may want to give yourself some time. Take it one step at a time and one day at time. Or if it seems right, do what you have to do and get it over with. You are in the driver's seat.

Repeating It 20 Times

I can express my needs and expect that people like to say yes eight times more than they like to say no.

Reflecting on Scripture

Matthew 5:14–16,23–24

The scripture meditation admonishes us to be a "light to the world." Jesus tells us not to hide who we are as Christians but to let it shine before all the world in order that the Father may be glorified. Often we can become so accommodating that the special light that we are intended to be is never seen. Each of us is a unique part of the continuing, unfolding revelation of Christ's resurrection. No one can supply our particular light except us, so we must let it shine. It is dangerous to believe that being accommodating is always the Christ-like thing to do.

Praying

Lord, help me to understand that the person I may have to forgive first, before I bring my gift to the altar, is myself, and that the gift that I bring is the "me" that you have created. Help me not to become so accommodating that I lose my unique self and the unique part of your revelation that I am. Amen.

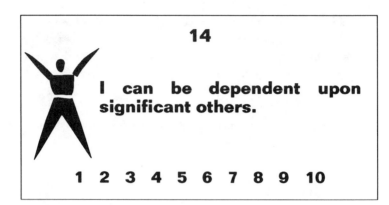

14

I can be dependent upon significant others.

1 2 3 4 5 6 7 8 9 10

Insight

Dependence on others can be an addiction. An addictive form of behavior hinders us from having a fundamental, positive relationship with ourselves—and consequently high self-esteem—and with God. An addiction is basically a substitute for being able to depend upon significant others. It is a state where positive relationships do not exist. It is what we use in place of such relationships; in fact, it provides an excuse for not having relationships, including a deeper relationship with God. If we do not have a positive relationship with ourselves (low self-esteem), it is unlikely we will have one with significant others. This chapter is about relationships that are not addictive.

Our ability to be dependent upon significant others means that they allow us to be dependent only in ways that are healthy. They encourage dependence but do not use it to control us.

Anchors That Allow Freedom

"Significant others" are the people in our lives upon whom we depend, those who mean the most to us and with whom we have a fundamental bonding, those who act on our behalf as something like an anchor, those for whom we are willing to pay a steep price to nurture a lasting relationship. They are the people we could turn to, if we were in trouble, and rely on them for help, no matter how difficult it might be for them. There may be no more than one or two or three significant others in a person's life. And to have that many is to be particularly fortunate.

Distant but Bonded

Our relationships with significant others allow us to maintain a basic sense of security, even though physically separated. There are those who have left home and significant others and traveled thousands of miles to get away from those they felt had too much control over them. In many cases, all that was accomplished was to carry inside of them the very persons they were trying to escape from. In healthy, dependent relationships with significant others, there is a foundation upon which we can build so that we can be a thousand miles away and still feel connected and comfortable.

As you consider who the significant people in your life are, one important question to consider is what you contribute in making these relationships truly significant. Not only must these significant others be there for you, but you must also be there for them in an ongoing and mutually nurturing relationship.

Misguided Independence

In our society we have fostered a false attitude about independence. We have made independence such an ideal that we have broken the bonds of dependence that are necessary to sustain relationships in communities. We must all be dependent and be willing to be such; it is the way we humans are. We must all have those we can depend on, and trust that such dependence will not enmesh us in unhealthy relationships.

Significant others might not be the people you would like to be significant. They are in reality those who make an important difference in your life and who will come through for you even though you may not care to admit it. Many people refuse to be dependent upon their significant others because they nurture a resentment toward dependence, which is based on their misguided ideas of it. Many are simply too proud to be dependent upon those who are gifts in their lives. Because of this "idealized independence," we are often not dependent the ways we ought to be and we don't recognize those who are ultimately meaningful to us.

Built on Sand

Many people waste a great deal of time trying to make significant the people who will never really be so in their lives. Children refuse the help of parents and employees refuse the help of employers, who stand ready and able to help, either out of embarrassment, a false sense of independence, or pride. We do not like to be needy because in a culture of independence, it is a sign of weakness. The plain fact, though, is that all of us are needy in many ways.

Being too proud or embarrassed to be dependent upon the significant others we have been given builds our house of independence upon sand—eventually it caves in. Those we think will come through for us really do not, and we must, with even greater embarrassment and perhaps humiliation, turn to those who are really our significant others and ask for help where we ought to have sought it in the first place.

Built on Rock

Being needy is not a weakness, but a strength. It is one of the ways we invite others into our lives, into our inner circle where we allow them to know us and form a relationship with us. When we begin to admit our need of others, we form a basic relationship with ourselves and discover that we need others to find ourselves. We also need God as a significant other. Living in relationship with significant others raises self-esteem.

When we share that neediness with others, we begin to build the significant relationships that allow us to remain in touch with ourselves and others.

This ability to recognize one's neediness is the first step in curing addictive escapes from self and others. The most profound escape in life is from a positive and healthy relationship with self, which diminishes self-esteem. For many rational and irrational reasons, we are afraid of this fundamental relationship, and when we begin to admit that we need others to be able to find ourselves and be in relationship with ourselves, we then begin to build a house upon rock.

Not admitting our neediness is a sign of that false pride that makes one the center and god of one's own world.

Moving Into Action

Ask yourself these questions and see what comes to mind:

Can you allow yourself to be needy, dependent upon others? What prevents you from doing so?

Write down the names of the people you would like to be the significant others in your life. Next, write the names of the people who would be there to help you, no matter the difficulty or what you did.

After each of these names, jot down a few instances when these people came through for you. You might note how they did this and how you felt about them and the manner in which they were present for you. Then reconsider who the significant others in your life really are and make note of the ways in which you have nurtured that relationship with them.

Answer the following questions:

Am I willing to acknowledge who the significant others in my life really are?

Do I have significant others in my life who are there only by my own wishful thinking, or do they actually deserve to be there?

Am I willing to be in touch with and to own my neediness?

What is my neediness?

What are the needs in my life that I cannot take care of by myself?

How do I feel about needing to be dependent upon others?

Do I see being needy and dependent as a sign of weakness?

other?

What did I do in response to being dependent upon a significant other?

Did I acknowledge the importance of their coming through for me or minimize the fact that I was actually dependent upon them?

Begin to recognize the real significant others in your life and make a decision to be dependent where you are truly needy.

Repeating It 20 Times

I can be dependent upon others without feeling less than I really am. Being healthy depends on sharing my real needs with significant others.

Reflecting on Scripture

Psalm 23

This beautiful psalm tells us what a significant other we are to God. It offers assurance that God is always nurturing a relationship that sustains this significance. It is, therefore, a model for sustaining the significant relationships in our lives.

Praying

Lord, I give you thanks for the significant others in my life that you have placed there. Too often I am proud and think I don't need anyone. Help me to humbly realize that I do have needs and that I am dependent on them for so much, as I am on you. Help me also to realize that they have problems and needs too, and to be alert to how I can be there for them.

Let me not shut others out, Lord, by pretending that I don't have needs or by being fearful that they will control me when I open myself to them. Grant that I may be aware of my utter dependence on you, and teach me to be dependent on those who can guide my life in such a way that I can discover the self you have created me to be. Amen.

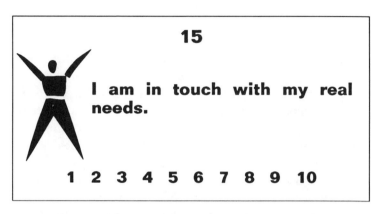

15

I am in touch with my real needs.

1 2 3 4 5 6 7 8 9 10

Insight

As a therapist, one of the questions I am often confronted with is, How do I know what my real needs are? How do I know if I am in touch with my real needs? Most of us are probably in touch with some of our real needs but are also deceiving ourselves about what our other needs are. We have only to think about those times when we really thought we wanted to do something, only to have done it and found that it wasn't satisfying, or wasn't at all what we wanted.

We have only to think about people we were attracted to—infatuation—and once we got closer we found that they were not as attractive as we thought, that they did not meet the needs we were carrying to that relationship. This may have happened so often that we are reluctant to identify our real needs at all for fear that they will not be satisfied and we will suffer the disappointment.

However, being in a relationship with our real needs is another way we are in relationship with our self and a sign of self-esteem. If we are afraid to be in touch with our needs for fear of being disappointed, we will also be afraid of being in touch with the real self that we are. It is important to believe that the Holy Spirit is within us, forming our needs, and that we can trust that ongoing interior formation. Over time and in prayer we can discern these real needs.

couple who had been married only a short
me that their needs were not being met in
either felt understood and certainly neither
was meeting their real needs. When I told
tnem that perhaps their needs needed to change, they were
quite surprised. However, the truth of the matter is that often
we are not only not in touch with our real needs but even
some of them have to change in order to find satisfaction.
When two people come together in a married relationship,
some of the needs that were satisfied by a single lifestyle are
not going to be met in married life; those needs have to
change in the new circumstances.

When we move into new jobs and into new circles of
friends, when we grow and when we change, one of the
things that most drastically changes with us is some of what
we formerly considered our real needs. We shouldn't fear analyzing and identifying our real needs, because we may discover that they're really not what we thought they were. Nor
should we feel awkward in admitting that something we
thought we needed wasn't really needed at all. The only way
to determine what our needs are is through testing. Are they
really "needs," or are they "wants"?

Verbalizing Needs

Needs and wants are often confused and there is a way, a test,
that often helps us to distinguish between them. We come to
identify and discern our real needs by sharing with significant
others what we think our real needs are. This enables us to
hear ourselves think; it allows us to receive the feedback that
others give us. Verbalizing what we think our real needs are,
getting them outside of ourselves on the table in a discussion
often results in a new view of reality.

People can share their experiences with us in such a way
that we come to realize that our needs aren't what we first
thought them to be. More than once I have shared my need to
do something or go somewhere only to have my mind radically changed by other people's experiences. When we share

what we think we really need, we will find our listeners m.
than willing to react; their feedback and questions are ofte.
quite surprising and enlightening. Talking about needs tends
to open people up in such a way that they are frank and honest with their responses. Give this a try.

Touching Real Needs
One of the most difficult areas to deal with in identifying real
needs, and one of the biggest reasons why people don't want
to do this, is because it may well mean big changes in their
lives. Being honest about their real needs may lead them to
have to make decisions that would radically change their
lives.

If some people face their real needs, they would, as a result,
have to make changes in their lives that would get their needs
satisfied. When we uncover our needs, we also have to face
whether or not they are being met. We also have to consider
our assertiveness—or lack of it—in meeting our needs or the
difficulty of the situation in which we find ourselves. Getting
in touch with and identifying our real needs doesn't mean
that our life situation has to change immediately. There is
much work to be done.

In fact, as you define your real needs, it may be important
not to change an unsatisfying life setting immediately. Other
people may depend upon us; we may be part of a community.
It may be important to give others time to come to grips with
these expressed needs, to realize that a change in our lifestyle
also affects theirs.

Remaining in a situation where your important needs are
continually unmet can be an unhappy one as well as unhealthy, but this can be changed over a period of time.
However, the question here is not so much the fact of change
or the manner in which it will take place; it is rather your willingness to be in touch with your needs. Many people are
afraid of honestly facing themselves and their needs for fear
of disrupting their lives and the lives of those around them.
Subconsciously they fear what they will find out. This is unfortunate because many times when people face their needs,

that their situation in life satisfies their
ley might have believed.

ompromises

re identified, it allows us to look at al-
.... and to make compromises, which are sometimes
necessary. Simply because our needs are not being met in one
situation doesn't mean that by altering the situation or radically changing our lifestyle that those needs would be more
readily met. When people begin to feel unhappy and suspect
that their needs are not being met, it is not wise to ignore possible compromises.

When we begin to come in touch with our real needs, we
have to ask where they can best be met or at least partially
met, keeping in mind the tendency to see greener grass on the
other side. When we face ourselves and our needs, and evaluate whether or not our needs could be significantly satisfied in
another situation, we can come to grips with stark reality and
define clearly how we can make compromises, how needs
may be fulfilled in other ways, and exactly how and in what
time frame change ought to occur, if change is called for.

It does little good to be afraid of our real needs and to live in
the fear that if we identify them, our lives would turn upside
down. Even if radical changes are required to fulfill our needs,
they can take place over a period of time and in such a way
that the pain is reduced for all involved. Too often unmet needs
are kept inside and left unresolved for long periods of time,
even for years, and then tragedy or large changes imposed
from the outside cause the situation to erupt all at one time.

Moving Into Action

Make a list of ten of your real needs. On a scale of 1 to 10—1
being "not at all" and 10 being "very much"—indicate beside
each need how much it is being met.

In another column, list concrete things you could do to fulfill the needs more effectively. Finally, list what you might ask
others to do for your needs to be met.

An important question to ask is whether you are presenting your real needs to others in such a way that they can respond to you and enable you to meet at least some of them. It is not selfish to own your real needs and to communicate them to others. In fact, it is selfish to withhold them because you deny others the joy of doing things for you. It is important to let others know of your needs and how they might respond to them to ensure both their growth and yours.

Don't run away from your needs. When you do, you are running away from yourself. Also, don't be afraid of finding out that your perceived needs may not be your needs at all. That can be an indication that you are outgrowing some needs and growing into new ones.

Repeating It 20 Times

I can have the courage to identify my real needs, and God will give me that courage.

Reflecting on Scripture

Psalm 89

This is a magnificent psalm on the faithfulness of God. Some forms of spirituality have made us suspect our own needs and have disturbed us if we felt we wanted to discover them. It is not selfish to do so, because they can identify how the Holy Spirit is already at work within us and move us closer to God. We can be assured of God's faithfulness as we honestly seek to identify and name our real needs.

Praying

Lord, you have created me a human being with real needs. Help me to know them so that I may be fulfilled and serve you and my brothers and sisters as you call me to. Grant me the courage to bring my needs to the attention of others so that I may find myself and you in them. Grant me also, I pray, the wisdom to identify my needs and, when it pleases you, the choice of being able to sacrifice my own needs for the sake of others.

And help me to remember that you do not desire sacrifice from me nearly so much as a contrite heart. Amen.

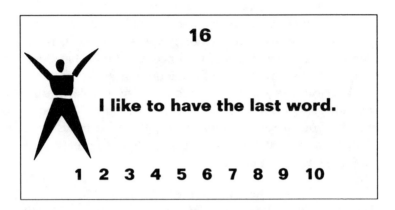

16

I like to have the last word.

1 2 3 4 5 6 7 8 9 10

Insight

Having the last word is a way of ensuring certainty and control. It is a compulsive, almost obsessive tendency that develops when you are not confident that people are thinking the way you would have them think. If you like to have the last word, you not only want to have everything neatly tied together and leave no loose ends, but you also have to have everyone think as you think and believe what you believe.

In fact, most of the people you allow into your world to get close to you are those who think and believe as you do. It's difficult for you to tolerate differences and difficult to have friends you think you can trust if they don't agree with you. Your idea of a conversation is a situation in which everyone at the table will agree on the same thing. The conversation consists of everyone adding to and stroking what everyone else says. What a bore!

Heavy Negativity

If you listen to your vocabulary, you will find that your sentences are full of "shoulds" and "oughts" and that you like to give advice and tell people how things ought to be. Very likely there is also a great deal of negativity about the condition of the world. Everything—society, politics, family life—is going to hell. Your friends and others close to you agree with you about this.

If you are not as negative as this and still like to have the last word, you may be in a position of authority in which you feel insecure, and having the last word is your way of assuring yourself that you have made it clear to others that you are in control. It gives you the security of believing that everyone agrees with you or at least will do as you say or think as you do. This is based on the irrational belief that everyone will stop thinking and talking after you have left the room. There is a fear that others will question what you believe or undo the authority you believe you have.

Liking to have the last word can be a sign that you don't really believe what you profess to believe, that you are unsure of being able to uphold what you profess to believe, or that you fear being unable to communicate what you'd really like to say.

The worst part about having to have the last word is your inability to allow others to really be themselves. Others must be what you need them to be, rather than who they really are. Liking to have the last word is a sign of intolerance.

Letting Things Dangle

One of the things that no one is particularly good at without practice is letting things dangle, tolerating loose ends. However, there are many times when it is important to allow things to exist in limbo and not be concluded. We have all been trained to set goals and to make decisions, and to finish a project within a certain period. This is believed to be a sign of progress, of achievement, but just the opposite may be true.

There are times when things need to dangle and not be decided or concluded. There are times when we need to leave a meeting with everything up in the air and nothing decided. There are times when everyone must have the freedom to express their opinions, whatever they are worth, and be allowed to have their opinions stand. People need the space to be able to disagree and to be in conflict with others; they need the space to be able to contradict themselves and to contradict others. It is in this milieu that as many ideas and feelings are expressed as possible, where everyone feels a sense of involvement and sharing, they are a part of the group. Every idea expressed affects every other idea and eventually, in time, sifts down to what is truth.

False Decisions

One of the reasons why decisions have to continue to be made over and over is because the decision has really not been made in the first place. A false decision— in place of a real decision-making process—was reached so that things look neat and tidy, cleaned up, and all business concluded. The world is seldom so simple. A person who is confident of her authority and of her ability to manage that authority can tolerate a wide divergence of differing attitudes, feelings, and ideas. In this situation, self-esteem is high and God's grace is not boxed in. Inspired solutions can more easily emerge.

This divergence of ideas not only contributes to an overall plan, but can pinpoint what can go wrong before something fails. It is important, then, to listen to even the most negative voice because even in that voice there is an element of truth that can keep a group or a community from making a wrong decision. "Getting all the facts" is more than that; it's also a matter of gathering as much information as possible to facilitate mature and encompassing thinking.

If you like to have the last word, you shut other people off and you abort healthy decision-making processes. Your self-esteem is low, and you are playing God. You create a situation where others avoid expressing their deeper thoughts and concerns, their real selves. You don't need to have the last word in order to be heard. What you do need is to consider the insecurity beneath your need to have the last word.

A powerful tactic with an adversary in a group situation is to get the adversary to say everything negative that he has to say, to get it out in the open, and then be able to say, "Let's all think for a moment about what Frank has had to say. We don't have to argue with Frank, or necessarily disagree with him. Let's just let what Frank said stand for a while and see how it affects us all." The silence that follows allows others, as well as Frank, to consider and reconsider what he said. When you always like to have the last word, you have difficulty with the tactic of allowing another person to speak openly or allowing a situation to reach its conclusion.

We are overly fearful of things getting out of hand and not nearly enough concerned with situations in which a balloon of anger and hostility may be blown very large. However, as the situation is allowed to ventilate itself, the large balloon of anger, hostility, and discontent steadily deflates as people freely voice their opinions. The process may be a difficult one, but once the balloon of disagreement is deflated, the facts are much easier to see on both or many sides of an issue. When you like to have the last word, you shut off an ongoing decision-making process, and one of the most important factors in the process, time.

In some instances time is of the essence in reaching a decision, but in most cases there is ample time to consider opposing viewpoints. If you like to have the last word, you probably create situations that make it appear as though there is little time to make a decision. Able authority does not fear other opinions and creates the time for input from others in healthy decision making, and does not have to have the last word.

Moving Into Action

Involve yourself in discussions or meetings in which you try to elicit the opinions of others who may differ from you. Practice drawing people out, asking questions of those who are silent or hesitant to express their opinions. When you feel compelled to arrive at a decision, check yourself and prefer to remain silent on the issue, and say, "Let's not make a decision right now," or "Let's all think about this for the coming week (weeks)," or, "Few things in life are absolute, so let's give this matter some time and see how we all feel about it in forty-eight hours."

If you like to have the last word, even getting these words out may be difficult and you may need to practice when and how you will express thoughts like these.

Repeating It 20 Times

I can feel confident and I do not have to have the last word.

Reflecting on Scripture

1 Corinthians 12:4–11

In this passage we read that there are many gifts in the body of Christ, and that they all work together in the Spirit and differently in their individual expression. If we believe that to be the case, then it will be difficult to behave as if we should always have the last word.

Praying

Lord, I like to have the last word. Grant me the grace to be open and really listen to all opinions and allow discussion and even contradiction to be part of the mix. Keep me mindful that your ways and your timetable are not always mine. Heal my insecurity, I pray, that impels me to want to have the last word. May all my words and actions, Lord, hasten your reign among us. Amen.

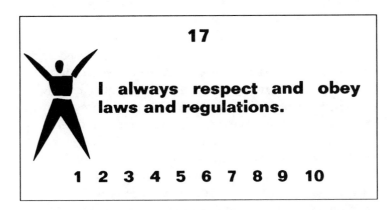

17

I always respect and obey laws and regulations.

1 2 3 4 5 6 7 8 9 10

Insight

There are times when laws and rules, because they are immoral or bad, must be broken. The term "civil disobedience" comes to mind. It is essential, though, that we respect and obey them. Without a respect for law, there could be no order in society. People who ignore laws and refuse to obey them exhibit a sociopathic behavior in which conscience plays no role. Often, a lack of respect for and obedience to law is a sign of a lack of respect for one's self. Respecting and obeying laws, which can indicate a high self-respect, can be seen in the smallest of acts.

The deeper issue at stake in this Inventory item is whether you *always* have to obey laws. There are going to be times when they have to be bent or even broken. There are not enough regulations in the world to govern every conceivable set of circumstances. In fact, the proliferation of laws shows that this is the case. What is important is to maintain the spirit behind the letter of the law. The discernment, or moral sense, that tells us when a particular law is to be broken in unusual circumstances is very important. Within the repertoire of our behavior must be the ability to discern when laws and regulations should be tempered by wisdom, prudence, compassion, and a concern for the common good. If we look closely at ourselves, we know there were many times when we have had to bend laws and regulations for others. All of us probably need to be more compassionate toward ourselves for having had to do so. The deeper our self-respect, the greater will be the compassion we extend to ourselves.

While it is essential to respect and obey laws and regulations, it is not possible always to do so unless we are using laws and regulations to remain in a dependent state. Always obeying them, regardless of particular circumstances, is a way of never having to come to grips with moral judgments for which we alone are responsible, with never thinking the matter through under the prayed-for inspiration of the Spirit of God, with never facing up to the promptings of our own consciences, which is the ultimate court of appeal. Blindly depending on outside laws and regulations because "I was ordered to" is to give our lives a false sense of structure and security. We meet many rigid people who act as though their very lives depend upon obeying laws and regulations. They so depend upon them that they have never bothered to get in touch with their own minds and consciences, which is necessary for allowing their real selves to emerge.

Moving into Action
Describe a concrete situation in which you are not certain whether the law of the system is the most prudent or the most moral way for you to act at the time. In another column, describe what you believe would be the more loving way to act under the circumstances, what you believe would show a greater openness and flexibility on your part.

Repeating It 20 Times
The greatest command is to love God and others. Sometimes I am obliged to break a human law to do that.

Reflecting on Scripture
Matthew 12:1–8
The is the classic story of narrow-minded Pharisees who accused Christ and his disciples of breaking the law of the

Sabbath by picking corn to eat. Christ attempts to teach the Pharisees that laws are for people, not people for laws.

The sheer number of law books on the the shelves of attorneys and the long deliberations of juries are clear evidence of the fact that laws of themselves are not the ultimate measure of right and wrong. There is a higher standard that in a particular instance may in conscience indicate that we have to break an unjust law in order to be moral and ethical.

Prayer

Lord, I thank you for the laws and regulations that give my life security and stability, but I also thank you for my conscience. I know you expect me to be sensitive to your law, the highest law of love, and internalize what guides me in my decisions. I may not ignore with impunity the conscience you gave me. Let me, by your grace, extend to myself and others the compassion that does not allow laws and regulations to hinder the growth you call us to. Amen.

18

I keep my anger under control. I don't let myself fly off the handle.

1 2 3 4 5 6 7 8 9 10

Insight

I have known many people in counseling who prided themselves on keeping their anger "under control." In most cases, their anger wasn't under control, but merely internalized, which eventually took on more destructive forms. The truth of the matter is that anger is not very well controlled in any form, because by its nature it is very difficult to control at all. Psychology has spent the last twenty years trying to get people to be angry and to express it, to realize that it is a good reaction to a perceived injustice. This was a reaction to a great deal of denial about anger, which needs to find expression rather than exist as repressed energy.

However, the deeper issue being addressed here is anger itself, and the realization that, in the first place, it is usually inappropriate, a needless waste of energy, and only one of many, many responses we can learn to make in a situation of frustration. We waste too much time and energy on it. We have learned our patterns of anger, so we can also unlearn them and develop new ways of responding to situations that upset us.

Don't pride yourself on keeping your anger under control; ask yourself why you have to get angry in the first place.

People who pride themselves on not "losing control" of their anger, on keeping it inside and never, never exploding—

at least not visibly—in reality explode inside and relive the aggravating situation over and over again. If you are always in control of your anger, never exploding, you are no better off concerning your health or in terms of self-esteem than those who "fly off the handle." You might think that "control" is a better way of handling anger, but if your response to a given situation is anger, justified or not, you might want to reconsider if never flying off the handle, expressing it forcefully, is really a good idea.

The concern of this Inventory item is for those who live by the principle that losing control is less desirable than controlling anger in another, more subdued, way. A habit of exploding in anger is certainly not a desirable or mature way of handling it. However, it is an inevitable way if you get angry often or if you hold on to your anger for a time, nurturing it. Anger demands a great deal of energy, which must have a release. In terms of both mental and physical health, if you get angry often and feel that you have to control your anger, it makes little difference whether you fly off the handle or not.

If you get angry frequently, you are going to lose control one way or another. You may explode only on the inside but you are still exploding, and the overall effect is likely to be no less detrimental, over the long run, than in the case of someone who simply lets it come out. In fact, this latter reaction may be preferable to more internalized forms of anger that don't deal directly with the situation that caused the anger.

Anger as Addiction
Anger, like most emotions, can be a part of a pattern of addiction, one of the early traps in an addictive pattern. We generally learn our anger responses from our parents and they probably learned them from theirs. Anger is not a response that generally reflects who we really are or how we really want to be as persons. It generally reflects low self-esteem and an unhealthy distance from God in prayer.

Anger can be the first step out of feeling oppressed and controlled by others. We can learn to rely on it to energize us to get moving. Then, when the anger wears out, we have no more energy to change or move. It can be the first burst of adrenalin that signals the larger escape down the roller coaster ride of addiction. Subconsciously, we may know that it will make us feel guilty and sorry for ourselves.

Anger is a habit that can be changed. It is a step in addictive patterns that must be changed if self-esteem is to grow and your positive self-regard is to increase.

Moving Into Action

Ask those who are close to you and those who work with you how you deal with your anger. Ask them if you get angry more than you need to.

If you express anger inappropriately, you are probably aware by now that you do.

Choose a way you would like to behave when you are angry. Practice the behavior in front of a mirror and watch yourself. Then, find someone that you can practice the behavior with. Act out how you want to behave. You may not like doing this, but if you really want to change your patterns of expressions of anger, you will do this exercise and find that it really works. You will also find that you have more than one way to react to annoyance or aggravation. You have many alternatives of behavior to choose from. Practice them, rehearse them with a friend.

One of the first things you will become aware of is that you will not always feel the way you are behaving; because of this, it will seem that you are acting. Your feelings are not your master. Just because your new behavior feels strange or your feelings don't match your behavior doesn't mean that you are acting or that you are being insincere. Quite the opposite. You have begun to let your thinking rule your feelings. Eventually, if you practice, your feelings of anger will actually change and new feelings that match the behavior will begin to emerge— but only if you keep going and don't let your feelings rule you.

The next time you become angry, catch yourself before or in the midst of expressing it. Stop short and change how you are behaving. If you can, actually turn around, physically half circle, to tell yourself that you can change your behavior. If you have to or want, explain to the person why you are doing what you are doing. This may not always be possible, but when it is, it will enhance the change in your behavior.

All of this may seem very difficult, but it is actually very healthy. Researchers of heart disease who once identified Type A behavior as prone to heart disease have now retracted overall Type A behavior as a cause of heart disease. They have made an important qualification. It is not the driven workaholic who is more prone to heart disease, but the one who is prone to quick outbursts of anger and hostility, and it makes little difference if the outburst is on the outside or on the inside. Getting angry and "flying off the handle"—inside or outside—is an equal risk for heart disease.

Repeating It 20 Times
I can choose responses to conflict or aggravation other than anger.

Reflecting on Scripture
1 Thessalonians 2:3–8
Paul is clearly disturbed by the Thessalonians. However, rather than show his anger, which he clearly feels, he chooses to be direct and to state his case. This is not always the way with St. Paul. Because he is human, we see him lose his cool, but this is not one of those times. He states his case and lets his audience know exactly where he stands; he doesn't keep it bottled up inside, and he doesn't explode.

Praying
Lord, I'm afraid of my feelings. I escape feeling controlled by getting angry. I can scare people away or scare myself away from others. Many times I don't even know that I am angry; I am just sullen and withdrawn. I don't "fly off the handle" because I don't know how and I don't know where I would stop, if I could. Why do I get so upset anyway, Lord? Why do I keep myself under so

much control? Why am I afraid of myself? Never mind the whys, Lord, just help me to realize that you have given me many ways of responding to life and that I can learn new ways. Grant me the grace to make the changes that will put me more in control of my feelings and my behavior. I pray for this. Amen.

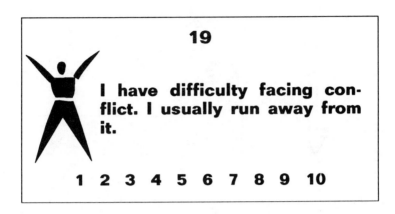

19

I have difficulty facing conflict. I usually run away from it.

1 2 3 4 5 6 7 8 9 10

Insight

Because facing conflict is never easy, running away from it seems an easy way out. However, flight can take as much energy and discomfort. "Facing" conflict and "running away" from it require equal amounts of stress and effort. The big difference is that facing a conflict usually leads to a resolution more readily and discharges negative energy rather than allowing it to build up inside.

Running away, on the other hand, employs defenses, such as rationalization, that require large amounts of energy to keep them going. Intellectualizing, especially denial, is a favorite defense of our times. Rather than face our feelings about a situation, we use the intellect to make excuses, to concoct a story we don't really believe, to deny our feelings. Energy is used to pretend that the problem doesn't really exist.

A Conflict Paradigm

The diagram on page 106, The Conflict Paradigm, gives a picture of the effect of defenses in a conflict situation.

Box 1 is what you would like to do; it is the drive, the steps you would take, to get the conflict resolved. It represents the

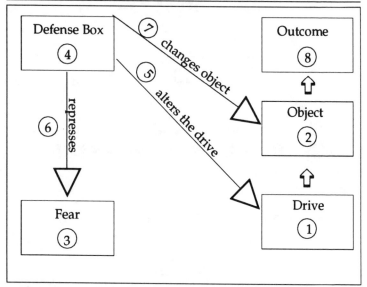

free flow of energy and problem-solving potential were it left alone.

Box 2 is the object of the conflict. It represents what needs to be resolved.

Box 3 is the fear of what will happen if you face the conflict: being overwhelmed, being rejected, and ultimately being abandoned by others.

Box 4 is the Defense Box. This defense mechanism tries to keep everything under control while doing nothing or as little as possible about the real situation. Requiring an enormous amount of energy, it must do three things to enable you to run away from the conflict. The first [5] is to act upon the original drive to alter the drive's nature in an attempt to resolve the situation. If the defense employed is rationalization, you might alter its strength by telling yourself that you really didn't want whatever it was anyway (sour grapes), that it really isn't worth the trouble and aggravation, and that you will just forget about it. Whatever the defense and whatever the message, the original drive is changed. You begin to want something else, or at least you try to convince yourself that you do. This can be the beginning of neurosis.

The second thing [6] the Defense Box does is repress the fear of facing the conflict (represented in 2). The defenses works so effectively that they even submerge the fear so you don't have to feel it directly. Line 6 represents the power of the defenses to submerge or repress the actual fear. This is one of the reasons why people experience anxiety. Defenses have repressed the real fears so that we cannot identify what they really are and the fear can only manifest itself as anxiety or worry without a definite object. After a while you end up not knowing what you want and unable to identify what you are afraid of. The result is the onset of neurotic patterns of behavior. However, the power of the Defense Box does not end here.

Line 7 emerges from the Defense Box and acts upon Box 2, the actual object (person or situation) and alters its nature. The words "changes object" appear on Line 7. If the object in Box 2 is a person who causes you difficulty and you end up not facing him or her about it, the Defense Box can send out a defense mechanism called displacement that will get you to think that the real problem is not your boss, but your mother. "Yes, that's it. If my mother hadn't done this and this and this, I wouldn't be in this position." And the next time you're with your mother you take her head off and then feel guilty later because you were unkind. Neither you nor your mother can understand what you were so upset about.

Defenses are power-houses of energy we use to deny and run away from conflict. This cycle, which is at the root of neurotic conflict, can recycle again and again and build patterns of behavior that are irrational and addictive. The pattern, or cycle, moves us away from a sense of the presence of God in our lives and creates anxiety and fear rather than the peace of Christ. Our self-esteem is lowered by the presence of fear and the sense of being out of relationship with ourselves.

Moving Into Action

Using The Conflict Paradigm, on page 108, fill in the following information:

In Box 2, describe a person, persons, or a situation that you need to face up to and have been avoiding. Use a separate piece of paper.

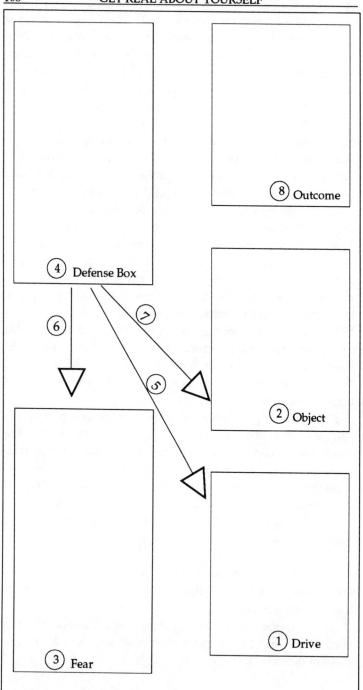

In Box 1 simply fill in these words: "My desire to get this resolved."

In Box 3 write down what you are afraid of if you really face this situation and come to grips with it. Write down your fearful thoughts and feelings. What are you afraid might happen to you?

In the Defense Box [4], write down how you think you can get out of facing the situation. What can you tell yourself or others that is in reality a rationalization? What can you tell yourself that helps you not to feel your real feelings? What irrational or illogical ways of thinking can you employ?

On Line 5, write down how what you have put in the Defense Box is affecting your "desire to get this resolved."

On Line 6, write down how you keep from looking at what you are really afraid of.

On Line 7, write down whom you might blame or what circumstances you might use to take your attention away from what you had originally placed in Box 2. How do you let whatever or whoever is in Box 2 off the hook?

And now in Box 8, write down whom or what you end up blaming. On whom do you out take your frustration? You might even put yourself in Box 8, and may well end up not liking yourself, or resenting yourself.

Now answer these questions:

•As a result of this insight, what or whom do you really need to face? What conflict needs resolution?

• Is this a conflict you can face on your own, or would it be wise to seek some advice and help from another?

• What are the most common ways you usually end up escaping conflict?

• Whom or what do you have a tendency to blame?

• In the end, how do you feel about yourself? What do you think of yourself?

• What decision do you want to make about handling conflict?

Repeating It 20 Times
I can handle conflicts and not run away from them.

Reflecting on Scripture
1 Samuel 3:1–18

In this beautiful story of being called by God, Samuel is thrown into conflict because he does not know whose voice is speaking to him. Eventually Samuel and Eli realize that God is calling Samuel, and Eli tells Samuel to let God do what God thinks is good. Would that it were so easy for us when conflicting voices are calling within us, throwing us into turmoil so that we often don't know what we're doing. Just like Samuel, we want to run from having to face the truth or from telling another the truth, as Samuel had to do with Eli. Our conflicts are much like Eli's: voices calling from within and often in dreams or in thoughts and fears, until there comes the vague realization that God is calling us to be or do or to say something.

Praying
Lord, I behave sometimes as though I'm asleep. I cannot hear you calling because I'm afraid of what I might hear, something I might have to do that frightens me, that I might have to face up to. By your grace, may I come to realize, Lord, that through the resolution of conflicts in my life you reveal yourself to me and I come to know myself better. I grow in and through these conflicts; through them your strength comes to me, and in their resolution I learn how to give back to your creation what you have given to me. Here I am, Lord. Amen.

20

As I look back over my life, things add up and make sense.

1 2 3 4 5 6 7 8 9 10

Insight

The Old Testament recalls the story of Lot's wife who, disobeying and looking back on the cities of Sodom and Gomorrah, and was turned into a block of salt (Genesis 19:15–26). Some people who look back over their lives turn themselves into blocks of bitterness and cynicism. They lack the capacity to look at their past with an integrative vision, that is, to see things accurately, in context, and with a willingness to understand and to forgive. Such an integrated vision of the past comes more easily to a person who has practiced this kind of acceptance.

The ability to integrate one's past does not come from an unrealistic remembrance of the past. It is interesting to hear people speak of the good old days. They are usually those who will tell you how bad they had it, and, on the other hand, reflect wistfully on "the good old days." Such a convenient use of the past is a cover for a fear of the present or the future. If the good old days were really good, they have prepared us to look with positive expectations toward the future and to also be able to live in the present. If the "good old days" have really been perceived as good, they become a kind of "whole" that provides a sense of grounding for the future. There is no reason to "linger" upon the good old days, because the present is more interesting and the future more promising, unless a lack of integration of the past has produced a fear of the future.

I remember asking my 75-year-old grandmother what she considered the one invention that most affected her life. I expected her to say the automobile or the telephone or air travel. Instead, it was running water in the kitchen. She explained that the water pump used to be in the backyard and that it was her job to pump the water needed into a bucket and carry it into the house. She especially remembered when she had to break the ice at the pump that had formed in the winter. She was not bitter about this, but recalled with pleasure the memory of something that was difficult and had improved, had become better for her and others.

I remember another time when our state was struck by a hurricane and we were without electricity for 10 days. The first day was fun and the family did things together we had not done in a long time. We went to bed much earlier and got up much earlier. The second day was fine as well. Then on the third day, everyone wanted to take a hot shower and my wife wanted to cook. We survived all right, finding a way to heat water and by using the barbecue grill. By the fourth day I realized that I had spent four days on what had become a survival exercise. It was and is difficult to believe the amount of time that went into basic chores and the little time that was left over for things we enjoyed doing. By the end of six or seven days, every single neighbor—who had first thought that being without electricity was so much fun—was exhausted and complaining to the electric company about how long it was taking to restore power.

We could have had a block party to celebrate when the electricity went back on. It is easy to take for granted how technology has made our lives easier and in many ways more "connected." There are those who would argue with this perception, and there is no doubt that we have not always made wise choices with the extra time modern conveniences have made possible for us.

Euphoric Recall

One of the reasons why unrealistic memories of the past exist is a phenomenon of loss called euphoric recall. When we have lost something important to us, whether a person, a job, or our youth, one of the ways of denying the loss is "euphoric recall." This means that a person denies the problems associated with it and remembers only the good, happy times. In some cases, a person will even remember difficult times as better than they were or completely distort the past and remember events that actually did not occur as they are now remembered.

After someone's death, what is recalled are only euphoric memories of how wonderful the person was. You may resign from a job or move away from a community, at first with great anticipation and relief. Several months later, you find yourself smiling as you recall the things you miss in the job or in the community you left behind. Forgetting the bad parts, you remember only what was good. You may also discover what was good that you did not appreciate, forgetting what you wanted to get away from. Euphoric recall is a part of everyone's behavior. It is one way to put the past to rest in order to get on with the present and the future. If the past has been particularly traumatic, euphoric recall can be an important defense enabling a person to get on with life.

Euphoric recall helps us to feel grounded in the present and to integrate the past in such a way that we view the past as "adding up," making a whole and making sense. We are able to see the hand of God and a plan weaving our lives toward simple holiness. It enormously increases self-esteem. Even the most troubled backgrounds can be integrated into the present. We must, however, decide to learn and grow from past difficulties. We have to choose between remaining bitter or cynical, and accepting and forgiving the past, realizing the ways we have grown stronger and wiser because of the experience. There is a gift that suffering gives that cannot be taken away: perseverance, endurance, and the confidence that we can make it through difficult times.

Dystonic Recall

The opposite of euphoric recall is dystonic recall, which does not allow the past to fit together with the present into a meaningful whole. Rather, it remembers the past in pieces that don't fit together, making it seem separated and fragmented. The past, then, doesn't make sense and doesn't seem to add up to any particular benefit for the present. It shatters a sense of wholeness and divides our ego strength among conflicts that have not been resolved. In dystonic recall we may dwell on a few experiences and replay them again and again as though they were a present reality. This allows single experiences or episodes of life to be all-controlling. We tend to blame and accuse people or circumstances from the past for our status in life.

There is a striking lack of forgiveness of others and of ourselves. We cannot forgive and go on because we have chosen not to. Remembering and rehashing what was wrong seems to be the only thing that will bring justice and assure us that the same will not happen again. A hallmark of dystonic recall is bitterness and cynicism, which does not make the present life any better. It can also be marked by a self-righteousness that undermines our sensory capacity, making our feelings suspect and over-intellectualizing a normal part of our life. The life of the mind can be exclusively valued over the life of the heart. Maintaining control over others becomes increasingly important. Healthy interdependence is often short-changed. And people with like problems gather together in clans and negative self-help groups that nurse and keep wounds open, rather than heal them and integrate them into a meaningful whole, and get on with a life free of bitterness and blaming.

Moving Into Action

Make a time-line of your past, dividing it into two- or three-year segments. Where there have been highs, or peaks, make the line higher. Where there have been difficulties and suffering, make the line lower. Do this a couple of times, as you remember more and more of your past.

- Where are the highs and the lows?
- What do the highs have in common?
- What do the lows have in common?
- At what period of your life were there the most highs and the most lows?
- Are there any particular highs that you use in a way that keeps you going today?
- Are there any lows that you continue to remember in such a way that they bog you down in personal relationships or in productivity?
- Do you need to share or talk through any of these high or lows with someone?
- How many of the lows have you shared with another person whom you can depend on to show you care and concern?
- How many of the lows remain secrets and things you would rather forget and not talk about?
- Do you need to resolve any parts of the time-line by talking about them and sharing them, being open to healing and forgiveness?

Memories and Forgiveness Inventory

This is an important exercise suggested for everyone who works through this volume.

Make a list of all of your negative memories by answering the following questions:

- What were my earliest hurts?
- What were my small hurts through life? (These do not need to be large or significant. We are sometimes influenced by the smallest hurts and negative memories.)
- What were the major hurts in my life?

Long-Term Exercise

Divide your life into five-year segments beginning with the most recent five years. List all the things that have hurt you. List anyone you have not forgiven. List anyone who has not forgiven you.

This may be a list that you want to work through with another person, with a priest or minister, or other professional. As you write your list or after you have completed it over several days, identify places where you still hurt, people you have not forgiven, and people who have not forgiven you.

If you are a religious person, I encourage you to pray about what you have written and to share it with another person you can trust. Perhaps that person can pray with you. Ask God to heal each memory and to give you the capacity to forgive.

In those instances where there are people who have not forgiven you, pray for them. You may want to go and actually right some wrong, or you may want to apologize and seek the person's forgiveness, but only if this is appropriate and would not cause damage or harm to anyone.

If you are not a "praying" person, you can make decisions and still act upon them. Talk through, with another, the memories that are still hurtful or cause anguish. You may decide to reach out to those you have harmed and seek forgiveness. You may want to let those who have caused you pain know that you want to forgive them and to move past the difficulty. Again, only do so if this would not cause any harm.

Decide to be open to letting go of hurt and pain. Our lives are filled with everyday "happenings" of healing that are life-giving. Healing can come through the circumstances of our lives and through the people who come into our lives if we are open to receive and willing to let go of hate and bitterness and to have our pain healed. The natural occurrences of everyday life can be healing and life-giving if our attitudes will allow us to see what is good in life and in others.

Repeating It 20 Times

I can take any experience in my life, no matter how negative, and grow into a better person because of how I will choose to deal with it in my life.

Reflecting on Scripture

Luke 11:5–13

Here we read the deeply assuring promise that if we ask, we

will receive; that if we search, we will find; and that if we knock, the door will be opened for us. The passage before this one is also important. It tells of a man who goes to his friend's house in the middle of the night to ask for help. The one in the house, after hearing all the knocking, finally decides that he might as well get out of bed and give what is asked for, not because the other is his friend, but because he will just keep asking until he gets what he came for. Persistence wins.

And so it is with us if we have Jesus as our friend. We will persist in asking until we receive what we seek, one way or another. One of the most important things we can seek is integration in our lives, which gives us the sense that our lives have meaning and purpose. This integration is essential for our emotional health. Persistent prayer helps us to look back and eventually make sense of the events of our lives and to begin to see the journey to God that is ours.

Praying

Lord, by your grace, grant me the power to forgive myself and to forgive others. Give me the courage to seek forgiveness from others where healing of relationships is necessary for all our sakes. I offer you the negative memories of my life, and ask you to release them. In their place, give me your light, your mercy, and your love.

Give me the grace of wisdom and strength, Lord, to let go of pain and hurt and of meaninglessness. Where there is no meaning, you can bring grace; where there is despair, you can create new purpose and meaning. Lord, you can make the experiences of my life whole. Grant me, I pray, the vision to see how you have done so already and that you will do so in the future. Amen.

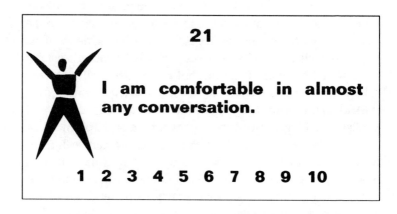

21

I am comfortable in almost any conversation.

1 2 3 4 5 6 7 8 9 10

Insight

Conversation is one of the primary means through which we reveal ourselves to others and through which others get to know us—our thoughts, hopes, desires, plans. It is also a way we come to know ourselves better. Ultimately, as conversations about political life, business, or the everyday affairs of living continue, they may become a signal for growing closeness and deeper intimacy. Being comfortable in almost any conversation is also a decidedly high indication of our self-esteem and a gift from God.

Another word for conversation is social intercourse. The very fact that we refer to conversation this way, using the word "intercourse," reveals it as a potentially intimate act. It can affect us in much the same way as sexual intercourse, as an exchange of attention, a ventilation and release of energies, and as a sign of giving oneself to another, allowing oneself to be known by another. It is the context of intimacy.

Anticipatory Anxiety

One of the biggest impediments to conversation is anticipatory anxiety; we anticipate being anxious, being uncomfortable; it acts as a block to the natural flow of conversation and builds up energy within the person. We anticipate saying something foolish or behaving in a foolish way and we fear being judged negatively or rejected by the other. Those who are uncomfortable in conversations generally are also uncomfortable with being silent, allowing the other to do the talking. There is inevitably an issue of control at stake here. Even though the person who has difficulty in a conversation has a great deal of anticipatory anxiety, that anxiety generally emerges from the need to control the conversation so that he or she won't feel awkward or foolish. That increase of energy is converted into more anxiety and acts as an even greater hindrance to being comfortable in a conversation.

Most people who are uncomfortable in conversations are also uncomfortable with what is called small talk, "cocktail conversation." There is no set topic or agenda, no prescribed outline of what to talk about. Small talk may seem meaningless and purposeless to some, but it is an important ingredient in getting to know others.

Many of the most competent and professional people, whom we would never assume to be uncomfortable in a social situation, are often quite uncomfortable in a social situation that has no set agenda. They may even describe themselves as being poor at small talk. Here, too, anticipatory anxiety emerges from a sense of having to control the situation.

The best way to become more comfortable in any conversation is to give up having to maintain control, handing the responsibility for carrying the conversation to the other person. When he has carried the conversation to a fair degree, the best way to take over is to ask questions about him and get him talking about himself. However, in all fairness, it should be said that people ought not to have to engage in every conversation simply to prove that they are capable and comfortable.

Don't assume that the art of conversation is a God-given gift for all; it may be a gift for some, but many others must learn it. In fact, most people have to learn how to be comfortable in conversations and how to carry them with grace and

confidence. Being a good conversationalist is a much overlooked gift in our time because we have not considered it
something important to be learned and developed. Doing so
will increase self-esteem.

Moving Into Action

Social Setting

In order to grow comfortable in almost any conversation, it is
important to decide explicitly, to make up your mind, that
you will be comfortable in a conversation by allowing the other person to take control of the conversation. The first step in
ending anticipatory anxiety in any conversation is to let the
other person carry the ball.

When there comes a time of silence, don't automatically
feel you must carry on the conversation; simply endure the
momentary silence. At first this will be uncomfortable and
you will feel you have to do away with the silent pause.
Instead, allow the other to be uncomfortable perhaps while
you give them time to think about what to say next. But be
fair, and don't expect the other to carry the ball all the time.

Before entering a conversation in which you anticipate being uncomfortable, particularly in a situation involving small
talk, memorize five to ten questions you could ask the other
person about herself. People generally like to talk about themselves, especially when the other really seems interested.

You may also want to ask another's opinion about specific
concerns, news items. After she expresses an opinion, ask
more of what she thinks and continue to draw her out:

"Why do you feel that way?"

"What influenced your viewpoint?"

"When did you begin to feel that way?"

Business Setting

It is important to define the agenda of the conversation beforehand.

List the points that you want to cover and the questions
you want to ask.

Write down specific issues that need to be covered, as well

as the information you need to obtain.

Don't be afraid to write down questions that clarify issues and set goals as well as time-lines.

Also, don't be uncomfortable about carrying these written questions into a meeting and referring to them. This doesn't make you appear unsure of yourself or inept, but rather shows that you are an organized, skilled person who gets to the point and gets a job done.

When you are questioned, give short answers, to the point. Also, once you have answered in a sentence or two, stop. Don't go on and on explaining yourself. Allow the other person to ask questions to clarify matters. Don't feel you have to add something else because you aren't confident that you were clear.

If you are uncertain you were understood, ask the other person what they understand you to have said; ask for feedback to make sure you have been clear. Keep it straight, simple, and to the point; let the other person go after more information.

Write down five situations in which you are uncomfortable in conversations. This is especially important to do. What do these situations or people have in common? Three of these might be social situations and two might be business. Write down the names of the person or persons you are uncomfortable with. Then write down five questions you could ask that person about herself and then add two or three more to each of them as a follow-up to probe her responses even further.

Practice asking these questions in a mirror, or you may even want to practice with a friend. Look at yourself in a mirror and get used to smiling. Notice how you ask a question, and practice ways to ask a question in a smooth and easy style. This sounds silly, but it works: Practice!

Repeating It 20 Times

I can be comfortable in any social situation. I have the ability to learn to be a good conversationalist.

Reflecting on Scripture

John 4:4–42

Conversation is very important in the gospels and is the primary way the gospel is spread. In this scripture selection, the Samaritan woman is astonished that Christ could tell her all she had done. She told others about Jesus and as a result many Samaritans in the town believed in Christ on her testimony. The scripture also tells us that Christ expects us to sow the word, even though we may never know the good that our conversations have created. Conversation, then, in the kingdom of God is very important.

Praying

Lord, don't let me use excuses for not entering into conversations, for not working to become a good conversationalist. Help me to grasp that conversation is a basic component of community and of mutual understanding. Through it, let me be part of building your reign in my neighborhood. I know I'm not the only one with this problem. Help me, by your grace, to make it easier for others to converse. Amen.

22

I've had enough of every-
thing. I'm fed up.

1 2 3 4 5 6 7 8 9 10

Insight

People and the events of life can get us down, or so it seems
at times. There are at least two responses to "I've had it." You
may have reached a point where you are no longer willing to
tolerate something that's happening to you. You have excused, rationalized, even forgiven without being asked; but
now you've had enough; you're fed up. Will you quietly withdraw? Or will you be a fighter and do something about
what's bothering you? If you're fed up, chances are you have
played out either of these extremes in your mind and emotions. You may have rehearsed a hundred scenarios of how
you will withdraw, or how you will explode. The question at
the root of either alternative seems to be how to get the most
satisfaction (vengeance?) from "punishing" the other party.
Neither alternative will increase self-esteem nor do they rep-
resent how God wishes us to be effective, that is, loving in our
dealings with people.

   If you are fed up with "everything," you are not focusing
your discontent on the source. You are focusing your discontent on being "fed up" and on what to do with feeling that
way so you can, one way or another, escape the feeling as
soon as possible.

123

Withdrawing

I have an acquaintance who disappears every time she becomes fed up. "Everyone will be looking for me," she assumes, "wondering where I am and whether I'm safe." That may have worked with her parents, and perhaps the first few times she tried it on other people, but after a couple of times it stopped working with us. She has grandiose fantasies about how she would punish us by vanishing for a time. After she exhausted her emotions or her resources and returned, she was disappointed and stressed again to discover that no one had really missed her. People had gotten used to her disappearing act and simply presumed she was doing it again. Many were just as glad to see her disappear because it became very frustrating trying to read her mind or her emotions.

Outburst

Not everyone reacts by withdrawing, and certainly not in the extreme way my acquaintance used to. Some people react by blowing up. This reaction is better than withdrawing. At least you let people know where you are. And, after a time, they will let you know that where you are is not acceptable and you will calm down and change your style. The people who will stay with you will demand that you change your style; others won't bother to let you "in" again because they won't trust you. Those who tolerate your emotional reaction to being "fed up" will use the guilt you feel afterward to get something from you. So will those who tend to be dependent and unassertive. Because you are ripe with guilt, you will give in. Obviously, neither of these extremes are good ways to deal with being fed up.

There are better ways. But first, let's look at the nature of "I've had enough of this and I'm fed up." This reaction does not usually come all at once. It takes months or years before it finally hits, unless you have an especially short fuse. We are so good at denying how we feel and rationalizing other people's behavior that it may take a long time to reach this point. If your slogan is, "It takes me a long time to get mad, but when I do, watch out," you may want to reconsider some-

thing before others have to "watch out." In the end, you will
likely suffer the results of your actions as much as, if not more
than they, whether you withdraw or explode.

Cumulative Oppression

Oppression weighs heavily on people. But often it can be handled in such a way that it does not add up to become op-
pressive. You may take each situation in your life and work it
through until you find a solution. You may generally manage
your life in such a way that you seldom feel oppressed. But
sooner or later someone or something comes along that begins
to get to you. It may be a person or situation you have put up
with for a long time. You have rationalized and you have forgiven, but now, rather than taking care of the situation, it has
begun to take care of you. You lose your usual equanimity
and everything seems to be too much. As effective as you
have been, it is not a single situation that you have to contend
with, but everything seems to have accumulated and is roost-
ing at your doorstep and you are fed up.

Strong, effective people can handle many sources of stress,
but everyone has a limit, particularly when it strikes their
Achilles heel. This attack on their weak spot is very dis-
agreeable and takes two or three times the energy to manage.
So far, you may have done pretty well, except for this particular stressor that just gets heavier and heavier.

Perhaps this source of oppression is another person you
have put up with for a long time. You have never really liked
him, but you have gotten along with him as best you can. You
have overlooked his idiosyncrasies countless times and told
yourself that not everyone is alike and that you must be tolerant. You haven't really stored your feelings to a point of being
hostile; you have been gracious and accepting and forgiving.
There comes a time, though, when enough is enough and you
are fed up with him; you feel anger. In fact, a good deal of
your anger is because you have let the situation develop so
long and have spent too much energy on it. Now it's time to
do something.

Before you do, at least get something out of the situation by considering these important questions:

How and why have you been willing to allow this situation to go on for so long? What has been the secondary gain? (One always exists.)

Has being tolerant so long kept someone dear to you placated?

Have there been material rewards?

Have there been advantages that you have allowed to outweigh what has aggravated you?

Where have you compromised, and why? (Somewhere along the line you have compromised.)

Was the compromise worth it?

Was it one that you will ever make again?

How did you talk yourself into "putting up with it" for whatever else you got out of the situation?

Would you do it again? Why or why not?

What have you overlooked or excused?

How do you excuse the same thing in yourself?

How can you grow from being pushed into a situation in which you feel fed up with everything?

The answers to these questions will give you important information about how you can avoid being oppressed in the same way again. In the end, only you can oppress you, and along the way to becoming oppressed, some of life's most valuable lessons are gleaned from examining how you got there.

Moving Into Action
Here are some common ways of dealing with "having had enough."

Delay Reactions and Plan Your Actions
Emotionally reacting to a situation that has caused you to feel fed up usually doesn't solve anything, except in novels and movies. Neither of them lasts long enough for the emotional reactions to wear off and the whole cycle to start up all over again. When you are fed up, decide that you will not react to the situation until you have talked out or written out in detail how you feel about it. Delay reacting until you understand

your emotions and they are out of your way and you can use your mind to maximum effectiveness. Don't hesitate to seek professional help on a short-term basis, even if the situation seems trivial. Counselors can help. So can talking to friends you consider wise.

Stepping Aside

Becoming fed up is like having to deal with a charging bull. If the bull is the energy of your own oppression and discontent, perhaps you need to become like the bullfighter and step aside. Tell yourself that you need to give yourself some time. Let the "bull" of your feelings pass. One or a few nights' sleep can work wonders with emotions since our dreams work to diffuse our emotions and conflicts. Resolve that you will handle the situation, but that you will not do so until you have understood how it works to make you feel oppressed or fed up. Resolve that you will not react emotionally until you understand why the cause of your oppression is able to get to you. Use the situation and all your past experiences and all you have learned to avoid being in the same situation again.

Stepping in Front

After you have figured out why you ended up feeling fed up, draw up a plan of action. How will you step up in front of the bull to confront what is causing the oppression? Talk this out with someone and get some input on it. You might also role play "stepping in front" beforehand. It is usually wise not to "step in front" until you have been able to understand and articulate why you feel fed up and have been able to put your emotions aside. It may be advisable to go to an adversarial expert, a mediator, and learn how to proceed.

When the time is right, confront the person by asking her why she is doing what she's doing. Ask her to understand why you have felt the way you have, and if she would consider this in the future. Assure her that on your part you will try to understand her actions.

There are times when waiting may be the wiser course and not be just avoiding the situation. You may decide to wait un-

til a similar situation happens again and then step up to confront. In effect, you want to catch the person in the act of doing whatever it is that has causes you to feel fed up.

If you know that others feel the same way as you do and
are fed up too, you may want to join with them and decide
when the best time is to do something effective as a group.
Don't waste your energy by not planning your response effectively.

Healing Both Sides

Much of this can sound like "getting back" at someone. That
is not desirable at all. In the movie *The Sting* there is the line
that suggests that the best way of getting even with someone
is when the person doesn't know that you got even. Let's take
that a step further. The best "sting" is when you won't allow
yourself to be oppressed in the same way again and when the
other party will never oppress others in the same way. The
ideal is to make sure that you avoid doing the same things
again that got you into a situation of being fed up, and the
other person will come to realize the advisability of modifying
his behavior as well.

Always try for a resolution that heals both sides. You may
not always succeed, but when that is the motivation of your
heart, you will end up liking yourself a whole lot more.

Withdrawing never helps you to find out why you became
fed up in the first place. Exploding sets up the same situation
all over again and you end up exploding more and more
because you get more and more fed up. Long-term cumulative
oppression, as well, is not resolved by either of these solutions. Oppression is an important teacher and a guide to freedom of the human spirit. Use the lessons of oppression well.

Repeating It 20 Times

Whenever I am fed up, I will stop and learn everything I can
and then proceed to be free.

Reflecting on Scripture
Isaiah 40:1–8

This chapter of Isaiah begins the book of consolation of Israel. If you are "fed up" with the difficulties of your life, meditate on this book and particularly these first eight verses. Here we read of the deep discouragement the Israelites felt during the time of their long exile; they are ready to give up. God responds with sublime tenderness, and calls upon angelic attendants to comfort them and to call Isaiah to prepare a way for them to return to the homeland that God gave them.

Praying
Lord, you love justice and demand it of us, but I have never considered that your justice extends to those times when I am tired of everything and fed up. In these times, help me to learn how you want to free me from any kind of oppression, what I put upon myself and what I allow others put upon me. Lord, may I not try escape from it with no consideration of your plan for my life. Because you do not work through a spirit of vengeance and hate, help me to realize that even being "fed up" is a time for healing, not for getting even. Amen.

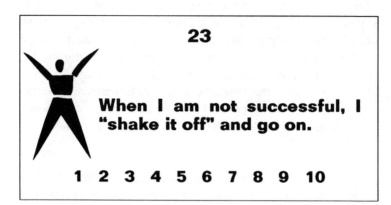

23

When I am not successful, I "shake it off" and go on.

1 2 3 4 5 6 7 8 9 10

Insight

Both of my sons are baseball players. The rite of spring is transporting them from practice to game, from practice to game. Baseball is a serious game, even if you're not playing for the Red Sox. Just ask my sons after they have lost a game.

I became interested in a phrase the coach used with the boys. Because doing well in a game was important, especially with their parents eyeing every move, they tended to "fold" and let down their energy if they made an error. If they took a particularly bad swing and felt foolish, the coach knew that the next swing was likely to be as bad because of their increased anxiety. And so he'd yell to them, "Shake it off." Pretty soon the parents picked up the call and whenever one of the kids made a mistake and got down on themselves, you'd hear the cry from the bleachers, "Shake it off. Keep going. Shake it off!"

Sometimes the kids would do just that, going through the motions of shaking something off. The physical gesture would redirect their attention from the mistake to playing the game. "Shake it off" was an automatic cue to stop looking backward at the mistake and to go forward doing your best.

This is a good lesson for life. There are some mistakes that you really don't learn much from except not to do them again.

If the parents were as good at shaking off their failures as the kids had learned to be by the end of the baseball season, their lives would be much easier.

If Only

Life can be filled with the sense that "if only" we had done this or that, things would be different. Sometimes, regrets are very difficult to forget, especially if you have been trained through guilt. (God is not a God of regrets.) Guilt training is a way of managing children by teaching them to feel guilty about a mistake they make. It comes from overzealous parents who do too much shaming, or who, themselves, cannot make mistakes. It can also happen in school when too much emphasis is placed on negative behavior and not enough on positive behavior. Guilt training happens when someone continues to blame themselves or others for something that went wrong long ago. Too strict religious training that is based upon fear rather than love can produce the same result.

A sense of regret can also come from a family, church, or social context in which a person is told in one way or another, "You can't be." For a long, long time this has been the lot of women and it still continues in some ways to this day. We have given males more freedom to be, in the sense of achieving and naming their own roles, than we have to women. Women were prepared for roles that did not include college and careers, positions of responsibility and leadership; they were only to manage a home and raise children. They were for the service of others.

When a person feels blocked in his or her being, there is a sense of the "regrets," which extends to all aspects of life and lowers self-esteem. Regretting mistakes becomes a way of life because there is deep, underlying regret about the nature of life itself and the choices that have been forced upon the person in one way or another.

Another source of regret and guilt comes from wanting to control things. Passive people who do not like to take risks, but nonetheless want things to go their way, are full of regrets. If only they had done this, if only they had done that.

And "I regret this" and "I regret that." What they really regret is holding out too long to make a decision to break the cycle, for fear of making a mistake. They will make a move only when someone else is involved so that blame can be shared or passed off to another. When these passive people do not make a decision and later regret it, they blame themselves and others for their own inactivity and then feel even more regret.

A great deal of energy is wasted in regret, in "if only" talk. Seldom is anything learned and the regret is a way of covering up the likelihood that the regretted behavior will probably continue. Like the young baseball players, if they do not "shake it off," they will not be alert enough when the next ball comes their way.

Moving into Action

Ask someone who knows you well if it is difficult for you to shake off mistakes or if you allow them to bog you down with a continuing sense of regret and guilt. Talk over with that person what you find difficult to "shake off." Make a short list and discuss with him or her what gets you down.

Shaking It Off

When you are alone (and others will not think you are going crazy), whenever you have a thought of a regret and begin to "if only" yourself, actually go through the physical motions of "shaking it off." Shake your arms or hands or body and tell yourself that you are shaking it off, whatever it may be. This sounds silly, but our brains also extend into our nervous system and throughout the body. When you have thoughts of regret, train the brain to think differently by arousing the neural circuitry in your body. Change the routing of nerve impulses in the body that are connected to certain patterns of thinking. Thinking differently and behaving differently physically in this way helps you make the change you're trying to make.

Mental Picture

When because of circumstances you cannot literally shake something off, form a mental picture of doing so, and whenever you start thinking "regret" and "if only," picture yourself shaking them off. Move your hands or your arm or legs in a slight manner, change your posture, redirect your attention, but every time you move into the "regrets," "shake it off" and get ready for the next ball that life will pitch you.

Repeating It 20 Times
When I am down on myself, I shake it off and go on.

Reflecting on Scripture
Psalm 103:8–10
Here we are told that God is particularly good at "shaking off" our sins. Would that we were that good to ourselves. Let's get as good at letting go of our guilt and getting on with life as God is at "shaking off" our sins.

Praying
Lord, I tend to give more attention to sin than to your loving forgiveness. Help me to realize that this narrow focus on past mistakes and sins only holds me back from carrying out your vision for my life; it hinders my potential for growth and being. You call me, Lord, to trust your understanding and compassionate forgiveness; that's the only way to deal with my past and to get it behind me. Too often have I used the past as an excuse for not taking risks and possibly failing. I pray that you give me your grace to live my life as fully as I can, for your honor and glory. Amen.

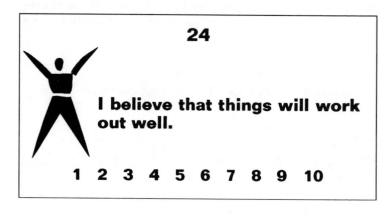

24

I believe that things will work out well.

1   2   3   4   5   6   7   8   9   10

Insight

Think about this Inventory statement. Do you really believe that things will work out well? People with high self-esteem believe so. When they really get down to thinking about it, most people express uncertainty, even downright doubt. Even those who ordinarily confess a great deal of faith, oftentimes express doubt when things aren't going according to their expectations. God can seem very distant.

You might think that life is difficult and that the suffering we experience and witness in life makes it difficult indeed to believe that things will work out well. The truth is that when we are willing to keep going and make the best out of a difficult situation, things generally do work out well.

While you might argue that you have a history of things not working out well, it is just as true that you have a history of things working out better than you expected. There are many times when events have surpassed your expectations.

There once was a cardinal from Venice who was getting on in years and wrote that he felt as though his life was pretty much drawing to an end. He had been faithful in his ministry, but felt that he had not really accomplished much. Life had been good and he had worked hard, but he had not had, in his own estimation, a particularly outstanding career. It was respectable and faithful and, in general, he felt that his life was pretty much behind him. A few months later this un-known cardinal from Venice was elected Pope John XXIII. Whatever the difficulty, "this too shall pass," and life goes on with the job of enabling creation to unfold. You may not become pope, but God has a plan for your life.

Trauma and Tragedy

It is particularly difficult to believe that things will work out well in a situation that has involved trauma and tragedy. There is a way in which tragedy cuts through hope at such a basic level that hope and trust can become impaired. One particular tragedy in my family changed things for a very long time. I had always been able to deal with death and with dy-ing patients. I had never found it difficult to visit people who were ill in the hospital. I was good at reaching out to those who were facing death. Then tragedy struck and I found my-self not wanting to go to hospitals, not wanting to reach out in this way. I would resist going to funerals and began to dis-tance myself from the experience of death as much as pos-sible.

I also didn't want to be so understanding, and for a while, as a therapist, I found myself taking a much harder line with my patients and distancing myself from their struggles. It was as if I did not want to hear anything more about suffering. I had had enough. I felt that something that had been alive in me had died. I became more fearful, much more attuned to the idea of accidents being possible. The possibility of danger striking began to seem much more real and imminent than it had ever been before. I also did not want "deep" experiences; I wanted to skate over the surface of relationships.

I knew that a part of me had shut down and I didn't even want to open it up. I felt for a long time that something so ba-sic had changed that I would never be the same. I had closed down to a part of life because I had lost a part of my trust. At the time, I certainly did not believe that things will work out well. I became much more aware that something could hap-pen unexpectedly, leaving nothing but tragic loss.

It took four years to put the pieces of a puzzle together so that the events made sense and I could to reach the level of understanding I needed to allow for acceptance. Often, we need time to make sense out of things that appear to make no sense. And even when they begin to fall together into a meaningful whole, it is not always something we can articulate. There is just a sense of knowing and peace.

Many people think that trauma and tragedy are resolved in a year or two. Actually, it often takes four or five years and more before things begin to come together in such a way that we can begin to trust life again, before we can believe that things will work out well. I believe that things will work out well, and it has been tragedy worked out over a period of time that has reaffirmed this basic sense of trust. God works through time to heal our wounded self-esteem.

Moving Into Action
Write down what you would really like to see happen to yourself and to others. Keep what you have written alive in your thoughts, hopes, and expectations. If you are a religious person, keep what you have written alive in prayer.

Repeating It 20 Times
I believe that things will work out well.

Reflecting on Scripture
Hebrews 11
This chapter of Hebrews is a sensational treatise on faith. It is difficult to find a passage in the Bible that is more filled with faith, more confident that in the end things will work out. Knowing that things will work out is faith in action.

Praying
Lord, what do I have that I have not received from you? You have given me, above all, the gift of confident trust and the gift of faith. It is your will that I use them well and, by your grace, give them back to you, developed and well used. There is nothing I cannot overcome with

you at my side. I can conquer any difficulty, any tragedy, even death itself, when I understand that the only
real failure is a loss of hope and will. Like your friend
Job, everything can be taken from me—health, intelligence, wealth, family and friends—but who can separate me from your love that will be sufficient to deal
with any situation? Amen.

25

I can make up my mind without too much trouble and later not doubt my decision.

1 2 3 4 5 6 7 8 9 10

Insight

Suppose you just received the following letter:

Dear Friend,

You have been specially chosen to receive this letter. Send a dollar to the next person in the chain and great riches will be yours. Break the chain and something terrible is likely to happen to you. A woman in Thailand followed these instructions and today she is a famous stripper and makes a ton of money. A man in San Diego chose to break the chain and fell in the San Andreas fault. Besides that, his mother and father were struck by a trolley car on a vacation to San Francisco and were instantly mangled on the tracks.

This letter has been everywhere and you must not be the one to break the chain. You may think this is just a joke, but things like this can come back to haunt you. Just suppose that you are the one to get the next round of dollar bills. You will surely get many, and you will avoid disaster if you don't break the chain. Will you be a link in the chain? Are you able to carry on? Send your letters today.

Suppose you make up your mind not to give in to super-stition and not continue the chain letter. How long would it take you to decide? How much will you think about your de-cision?

Many people would say that they would throw it in the trash, but we really don't know what most people would do. Judging from the number of chain letters that circulate each year, it appears there are a lot of people who don't really be-lieve in chain letters, but answer them "just in case."

How difficult is it for you to make up your mind and to carry out what you have decided to do without doubting your decision? Have you ever felt "buyer's regret," the feeling that comes after you have bought something for a good deal of money but before you get to see what you have purchased ac-tually delivered?

A certain amount of doubt is going to follow decision mak-ing. The more important the decision, the greater the potential doubt. You should not be surprised to find yourself doubting what you may have decided. The question is whether the doubt is appropriate and proportionate to the decision.

Lack of Cultural Realism

I recently read the following in the Sunday magazine of the *New York Times:*

> The breeze caresses a wind chime. Near the French doors, a man stands framed by billowing curtains. Cut to a woman, spraying on perfume. Cut to the man and woman together, kissing. Back to the man, alone, dream-ily inhaling the scent of his beloved's letter. He looks out, and there she is, in a car below. Smiles all around. Cut to a bottle of Prince Matchabelli's Wind Song per-fume. In the background, romantic music and a whis-pered message: "I can't seem to forget you. Your Wind Song stays on my mind."

For the past two years both my wife and I have forgotten our anniversary. If it weren't for my mother-in-law's faithful cards to remind us, we probably would not have realized we had missed "our day" until summer was over. Last year my wife and I were confident we would remember to observe our anniversary. We were aware of it weeks and days beforehand. Well, I went off to a soccer tournament with my son and expected to be home in a day because the feeling was that his team would lose the first day or at least by the second. Needless to say, his team went undefeated and I spent our anniversary in a hotel room washing socks and soccer shirts in the hotel sink, while my son and his teammates dropped my quarters into the video arcade, rested, and got "psyched" for the next day's game.

The distance between Wind Song and that soccer tournament, between reality and romantic fantasy, is a trillion miles. Here I am at a soccer tournament on my anniversary and somebody broadcasts this nonsense about some perfume.

Reality Gap

There is a reality gap between most of the repetitive hype constantly cast before us and what life is really about. This cultural reality gap makes decisions even more difficult. Again and again, precisely this kind of Wind Song hype saturates our society, and we wonder about our mundane lives with their daily-grind decisions. I had made up my mind to go to this soccer game—a perfectly reasonable decision at the time—as many of you have made up your minds to be parents or managers or poets or teachers. But there is not much in our culture which tells us that life as we live it every day is really life as it ought to be.

When we begin to doubt our reality, it is very difficult to make decisions and later not doubt them. There are many people who doubt their reality and this undermines their capacity to make a decision and then, regardless of the outcome, go forward. There are too many people regretting too many decisions because they've been absorbing too much Wind Song philosophy. We have to determine that our decisions will be based on what is really important to us.

The "Trophy"

My son and I drove home with his trophy at the end of the third day. I was hoarse from yelling and my legs ached because there were no bleachers and I had forgotten to bring a lawn chair. We talked and replayed the game and shared the sweet smell of winning at 14 years old when you weren't supposed to.

Before long, you will probably see a commercial, featuring a father and a son at a soccer tournament, selling shoes or cologne or lawn chairs. It will be the perfect commercial with perfect weather. (It had rained during half the tournament and the players were covered with mud, but that part won't be there.) And the commercial won't mention missing your anniversary or whatever you have to miss when you make a decision that takes you in some direction that matters. If you measure your experience at that soccer tournament against the Wind Song commercial, you lose. If you remember how life really is with the well-intentioned decisions you make day after day, you win.

There is much in society that does not help you make decisions in a meaningful way. In fact, there's much that assumes you don't have a mind at all. And too often, this lack of a realistic outlook on life militates against our making decisions without too much trouble and later not doubting or regretting them.

Only you and the relationships in your life can help you decide what is real and meaningful for you. Decide to decide, do so with reasonable confidence, and find and maintain the relationships that can sustain you when you are wrong and celebrate with you when you are right. God will bless your well-intended decision making, and your self-esteem will increase.

Moving Into Action

Write out a list of the five top priorities in your life. In the column opposite, try to describe how each priority will influence typical decisions you will likely have to make.

If you are having a difficult time, this next assignment may be very difficult, but it can be very life-giving. Visit or volunteer to work at a hospice or a children's hospital. If you have the courage, talk to those who are dying. As we deny the reality of death, we move further and further away from being able to make important decisions in the light of our priorities, and to avoid irrational doubt.

Repeating It 20 Times

I will prize life and decide where mine is going. I will make the decisions that will take me there and I won't look back.

Reflecting on Scripture

Matthew 6:21

Your treasure—values—is where your heart is. When we know where our heart is, when we know what is really important to us, making decisions is much easier. We will know what our direction is. But our treasure, or at least our knowledge of it, can be eroded by a media world full of messages that can lead us away from our treasure and our ability to decide for it.

Praying

Lord, I sometimes sell out to an idea of reality that is pumped at me from all sides. Sometimes I want to be the person in the billboard rather than myself. I do so much to go along with the crowd and I worry so much about what the neighbors will think. Lord, you have a purpose and meaning for my life.

May I, with your grace, hear your call and develop this vision for my life that is flexible enough when I seek to give back to you what you have given to me. Help me, I pray, to head straight for it in all my decisions. They won't always, in hindsight, be the right decisions, but let me realize that at the time I made them with your love in mind. Amen.

Resources

Benson, Herbert. *The Relaxation Response.* New York: William Morrow, 1976.

Berglas, Steven. *The Success Syndrome.* New York: Plenum Press, 1986.

Burns, David D. *Feeling Good.* New York: William Morrow, 1980.

Carnes, Patrick. *Out of the Shadows.* Minneapolis: CompCare Publishers, 1983.

Johnson, Robert A. *He!* King of Prussia, PA: Religious Publishing Co., 1974.

_____. *She!* King of Prussia, PA: Religious Publishing Co., 1976.

Johnson, Spencer. *One Minute for Myself.* New York: William Morrow, 1985.

Keating, Thomas. *Open Mind, Open Heart.* Warwick, NY: Amity House, 1986.

Kiley, Dan. *The Peter Pan Syndrome.* New York: Dodd, Mead, 1983.

Kübler-Ross, Elisabeth. *On Death and Dying.* New York: Macmillan, 1969.

Larkin, William K. *Breakthrough With Dr. Larkin.*
Conquering Worry.
Everyday Addictions.

Focus Your Heart.

Healing: Integrating Psychology and Religion.

The Hermits.

The Humility of Self-Esteem.

I Am Myself.

Mary, Gift Us With Trust.

Our Friends on Wooster Square.

Rainbow.

*The Self-Esteem Manual.**

Levis, Albert J. *Conflict Analysis: The Formal Theory of Behavior.* Manchester Village, VT: Normative Publications, 1988.

Linn, Matthew and Dennis. *Healing Life's Hurts.* New York/ Ramsey, NJ: Paulist Press, 1978.

Luscher, Max. *The Four-Color Person.* New York: Simon and Schuster, 1979.

Mahl, George. *Psychological Conflict and Defense.* New York: Harcourt, Brace, Jovanovich, 1971.

Marks, Isaac. *Living With Fear.* New York: McGraw Hill, 1978.

Metz, Johannes. *Poverty of Spirit.* New York: Paulist Press, 1968.

Nathan, Ronald G., Thomas E. Staats, and Paul J. Rosch. *The Doctors' Guide to Instant Stress Relief.* New York: G.P. Putnam's Sons, 1987.

Pearsall, Paul. *Super Immunity.* New York: Ballantine Books, 1987.

_____. *Super Joy.* New York: Doubleday, 1988.

Rosenthal, Robert, and Lenore Jacobson. *Pygmalion in the Classroom,* New York: Irvington Press, 1988.

Sanford, Agnes. *Healing Gifts of the Spirit.* New York: Harper & Row, 1984.

Stroebel, Charles. *Quieting Reflex Training for Adults.* New York: BMA Audio Cassette Publications, 1983.

*Resources by Dr. Larkin can be obtained by writing to Box 6177, Hamden, CT 06517, or by calling 1-203-281-6593. Other resources are available at better book stores.

The Self-Esteem Seminar
or 3 other seminars,
Conquering Worry and Stress
Transitions
The Second Half of Life

can be booked for your group by writing to

Dr. Larkin
Box 6177
Hamden, CT 06517
or by calling
203-281-6593

Of Related Interest...

God Delights in You
A Four-Week Prayer Journal for Busy Christians
Bridget Mary Meehan
Offered are quotes from Scripture and Christian mystics, reflections
on a specific weekly theme and individual prayer experiences that
can be used throughout the day—all leading to a richer prayer life.
ISBN: 0-89622-603-4, 128 pp, $7.95

Scripture Reflections Day by Day
Rev. Joseph G. Donders
These 365 meditations are current, timely, short enough to be read in
any free moment and full of meaning and hope in a fragmented
world.
ISBN: 0-89622-494-5, 384 pp, $9.95

An Enneagram Guide
A Spirituality of Love in Brokenness
Éilís Bergin and Eddie Fitzgerald
Here is a concise overview of the Enneagram: its history and how it
can help people today. Presents characteristics of the personality
types and information on spiritual development for each.
ISBN: 0-89622-564-X, 128 pp, $8.95

Who We Are Is How We Pray
Charles Keating
Draws on the 16 personality types in the Myers-Briggs personality
inventory and matches each to a style of spirituality.
ISBN: 0-89622-321-3, 168 pp, $7.95

Available at religious bookstores or from
TWENTY-THIRD PUBLICATIONS
P.O. Box 180 • Mystic, CT 06355
1-800-321-0411

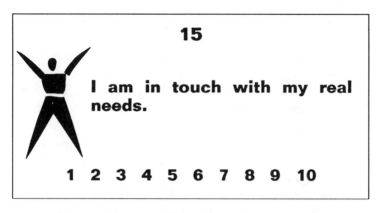

15

I am in touch with my real needs.

1 2 3 4 5 6 7 8 9 10

Insight

As a therapist, one of the questions I am often confronted with is, How do I know what my real needs are? How do I know if I am in touch with my real needs? Most of us are probably in touch with some of our real needs but are also deceiving ourselves about what our other needs are. We have only to think about those times when we really thought we wanted to do something, only to have done it and found that it wasn't satisfying, or wasn't at all what we wanted.

We have only to think about people we were attracted to—infatuation—and once we got closer we found that they were not as attractive as we thought, that they did not meet the needs we were carrying to that relationship. This may have happened so often that we are reluctant to identify our real needs at all for fear that they will not be satisfied and we will suffer the disappointment.

However, being in a relationship with our real needs is another way we are in relationship with our self and a sign of self-esteem. If we are afraid to be in touch with our needs for fear of being disappointed, we will also be afraid of being in touch with the real self that we are. It is important to believe that the Holy Spirit is within us, forming our needs, and that we can trust that ongoing interior formation. Over time and in prayer we can discern these real needs.

Changing Needs

Some time ago, a couple who had been married only a short time admitted to me that their needs were not being met in their marriage. Neither felt understood and certainly neither felt that the other was meeting their real needs. When I told them that perhaps their needs needed to change, they were quite surprised. However, the truth of the matter is that often we are not only not in touch with our real needs but even some of them have to change in order to find satisfaction. When two people come together in a married relationship, some of the needs that were satisfied by a single lifestyle are not going to be met in married life; those needs have to change in the new circumstances.

When we move into new jobs and into new circles of friends, when we grow and when we change, one of the things that most drastically changes with us is some of what we formerly considered our real needs. We shouldn't fear analyzing and identifying our real needs, because we may discover that they're really not what we thought they were. Nor should we feel awkward in admitting that something we thought we needed wasn't really needed at all. The only way to determine what our needs are is through testing. Are they really "needs," or are they "wants"?

Verbalizing Needs

Needs and wants are often confused and there is a way, a test, that often helps us to distinguish between them. We come to identify and discern our real needs by sharing with significant others what we think our real needs are. This enables us to hear ourselves think; it allows us to receive the feedback that others give us. Verbalizing what we think our real needs are, getting them outside of ourselves on the table in a discussion often results in a new view of reality.

People can share their experiences with us in such a way that we come to realize that our needs aren't what we first thought them to be. More than once I have shared my need to do something or go somewhere only to have my mind radically changed by other people's experiences. When we share what we think we really need, we will find our listeners more than willing to react; their feedback and questions are often quite surprising and enlightening. Talking about needs tends to open people up in such a way that they are frank and honest with their responses. Give this a try.

Touching Real Needs
One of the most difficult areas to deal with in identifying real needs, and one of the biggest reasons why people don't want to do this, is because it may well mean big changes in their lives. Being honest about their real needs may lead them to have to make decisions that would radically change their lives.

If some people face their real needs, they would, as a result, have to make changes in their lives that would get their needs satisfied. When we uncover our needs, we also have to face whether or not they are being met. We also have to consider our assertiveness—or lack of it—in meeting our needs or the difficulty of the situation in which we find ourselves. Getting in touch with and identifying our real needs doesn't mean that our life situation has to change immediately. There is much work to be done.

In fact, as you define your real needs, it may be important not to change an unsatisfying life setting immediately. Other people may depend upon us; we may be part of a community. It may be important to give others time to come to grips with these expressed needs, to realize that a change in our lifestyle also affects theirs.

Remaining in a situation where your important needs are continually unmet can be an unhappy one as well as unhealthy, but this can be changed over a period of time. However, the question here is not so much the fact of change or the manner in which it will take place; it is rather your willingness to be in touch with your needs. Many people are afraid of honestly facing themselves and their needs for fear of disrupting their lives and the lives of those around them. Subconsciously they fear what they will find out. This is unfortunate because many times when people face their needs,

what they find is that their situation in life satisfies their
needs more than they might have believed.

Alternatives and Compromises
Once real needs are identified, it allows us to look at alternatives and to make compromises, which are sometimes
necessary. Simply because our needs are not being met in one
situation doesn't mean that by altering the situation or radically changing our lifestyle that those needs would be more
readily met. When people begin to feel unhappy and suspect
that their needs are not being met, it is not wise to ignore possible compromises.

When we begin to come in touch with our real needs, we
have to ask where they can best be met or at least partially
met, keeping in mind the tendency to see greener grass on the
other side. When we face ourselves and our needs, and evaluate whether or not our needs could be significantly satisfied in
another situation, we can come to grips with stark reality and
define clearly how we can make compromises, how needs
may be fulfilled in other ways, and exactly how and in what
time frame change ought to occur, if change is called for.

It does little good to be afraid of our real needs and to live in
the fear that if we identify them, our lives would turn upside
down. Even if radical changes are required to fulfill our needs,
they can take place over a period of time and in such a way
that the pain is reduced for all involved. Too often unmet needs
are kept inside and left unresolved for long periods of time,
even for years, and then tragedy or large changes imposed
from the outside cause the situation to erupt all at one time.

Moving Into Action
Make a list of ten of your real needs. On a scale of 1 to 10—1
being "not at all" and 10 being "very much"—indicate beside
each need how much it is being met.

In another column, list concrete things you could do to fulfill the needs more effectively. Finally, list what you might ask
others to do for your needs to be met.

An important question to ask is whether you are pre-